EASY PIANO

FIRST 50
POPULAR SONGS
YOU SHOULD PLAY ON THE PIANO

ISBN 978-1-4803-9802-3

Visit Hal Leonard Online at
www.halleonard.com

World headquarters, contact:
Hal Leonard
7777 West Bluemound Road
Milwaukee, WI 53213
Email: info@halleonard.com

In Europe, contact:
Hal Leonard Europe Limited
1 Red Place
London, W1K 6PL
Email: info@halleonardeurope.com

In Australia, contact:
Hal Leonard Australia Pty. Ltd.
4 Lentara Court
Cheltenham, Victoria, 3192 Australia
Email: info@halleonard.com.au

AGAINST THE WIND

Words and Music by
BOB SEGER

Medium Rock beat

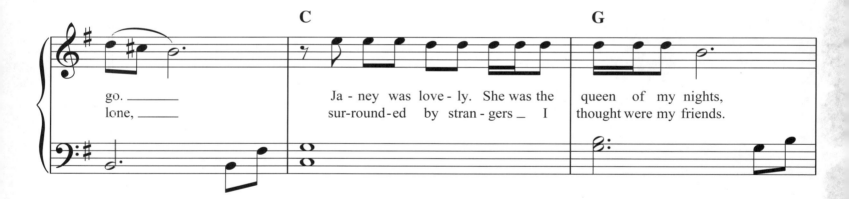

It seems like yes-ter - day, but it was long a -
And the years rolled slow - ly past. And I found my - self a -
Instrumental solo

go. _____ Ja - ney was love - ly. She was the queen of my nights,
lone, _____ sur-round-ed by stran - gers _ I thought were my friends.

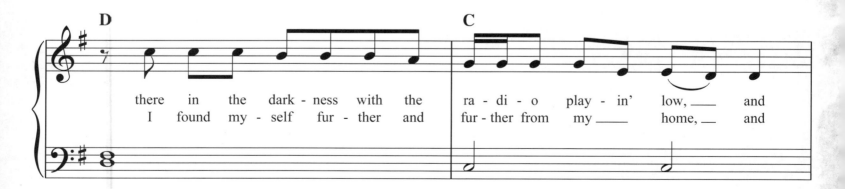

there in the dark - ness with the ra - di - o play - in' low, ____ and
I found my - self fur - ther and fur - ther from my ____ home, ____ and

the se-crets that we shared,
I guess I lost my way.

the moun-tains that we moved, _
There were oh, so man-y roads, __

I was

caught like a wild-fire out of con-
liv-in' to run and run-nin' to

trol _____
live. _____

till there was
Nev-er

noth-in' left to burn and noth-in' left to
wor-ried about pay-in', or e-ven how much I

prove. _____
owed. _____
End instrumental solo

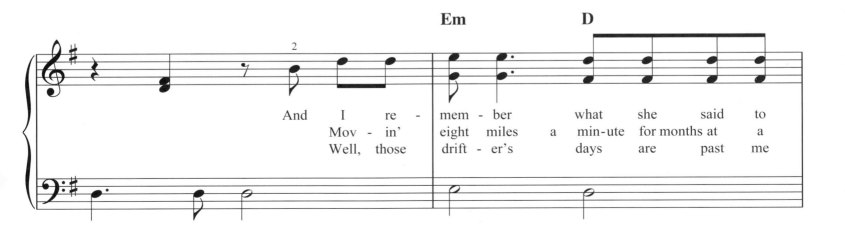

And I re-
Mov-in'
Well, those

mem-ber
eight miles
drift-er's

what
a min-ute
days

she said to
for months at a
are past me

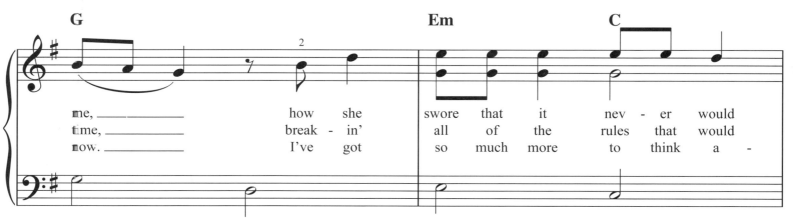

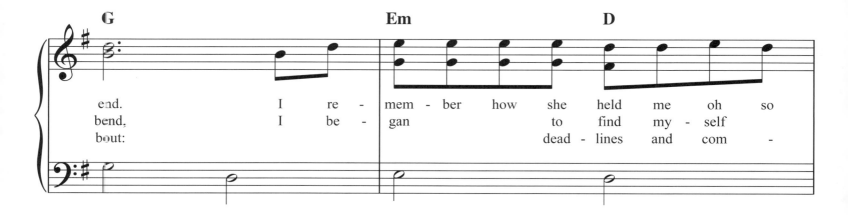

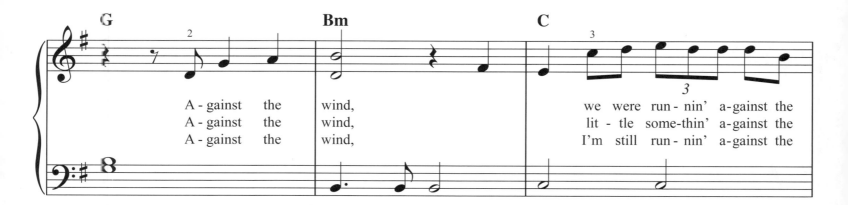

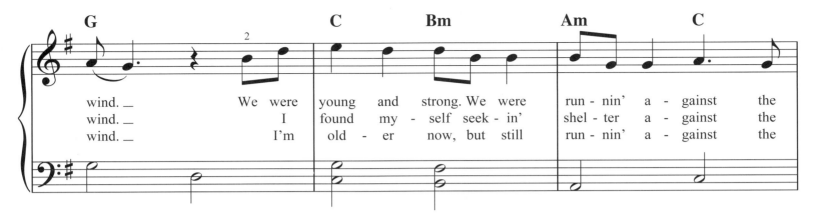

wind. _   We were young and strong. We were runnin' a - gainst the
wind. _   I found my - self seek - in' shel - ter a - gainst the
wind. _   I'm old - er now, but still run - nin' a - gainst the

wind.
wind.
wind.

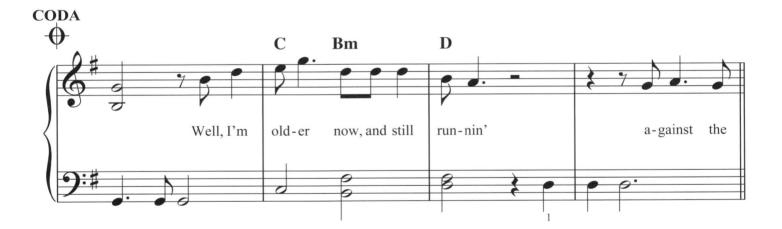

Well, I'm old-er now, and still runnin' a-gainst the

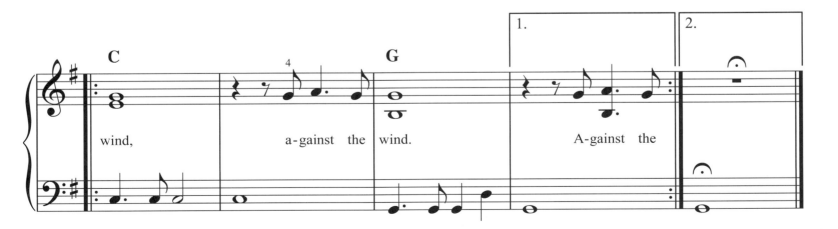

wind, a-gainst the wind. A-gainst the

ANGEL

Words and Music by
SARAH McLACHLAN

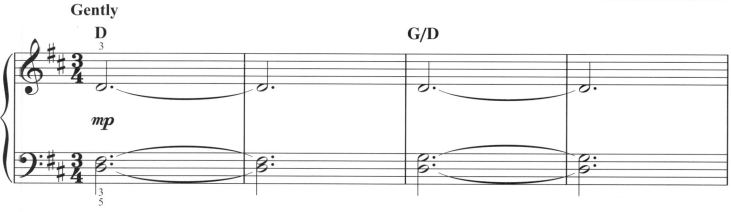

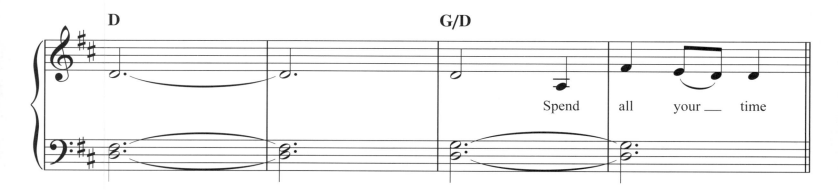

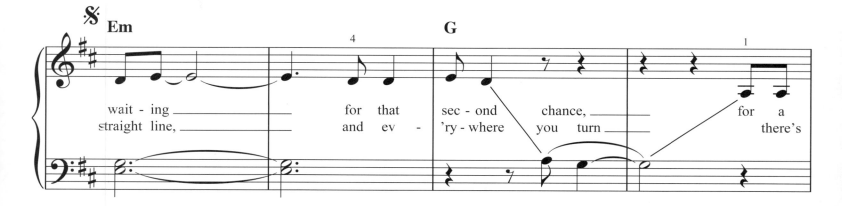

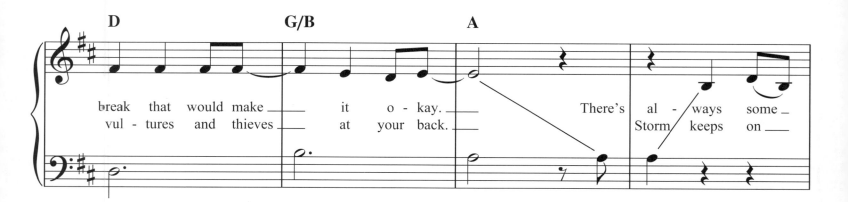

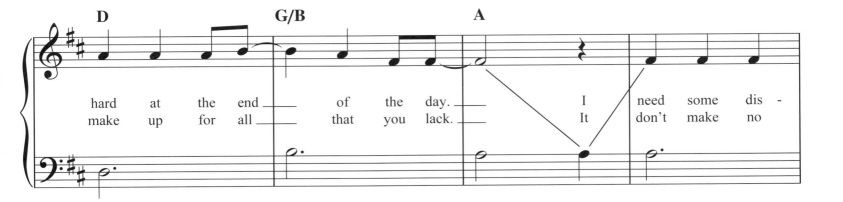

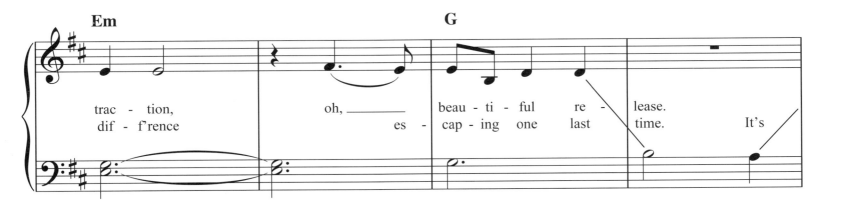

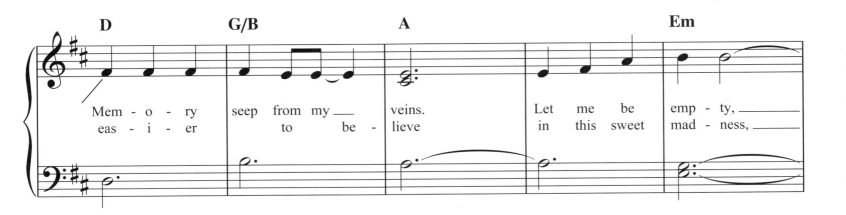

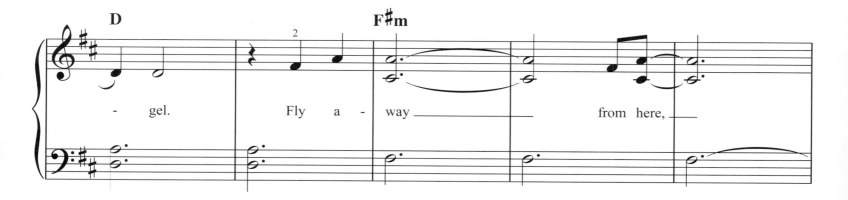

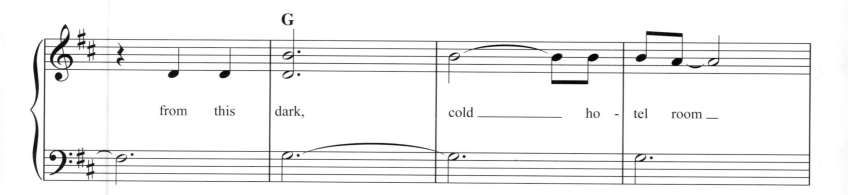

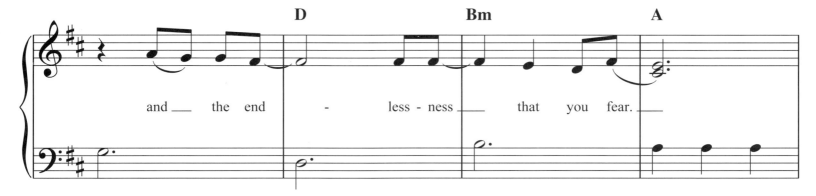

and ___ the end - less - ness ___ that you fear. ___

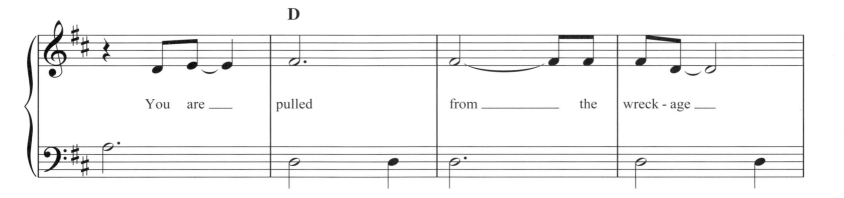

You are ___ pulled from ___ the wreck - age ___

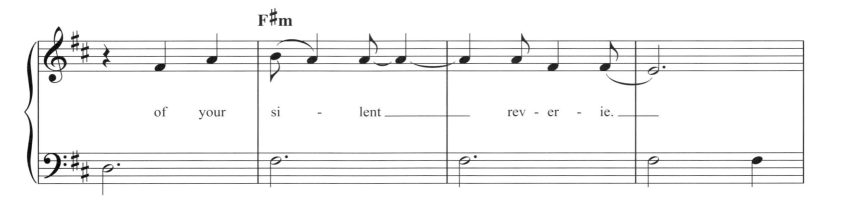

of your si - lent ___ rev - er - ie. ___

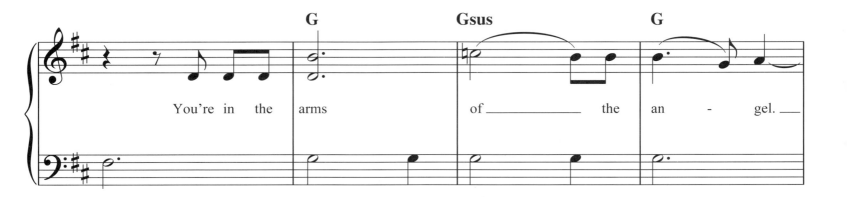

You're in the arms of ___ the an - gel. ___

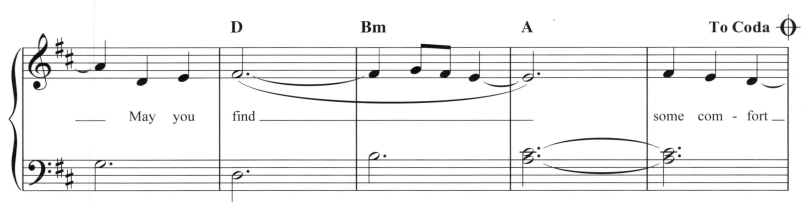

May you find _____ some com - fort _

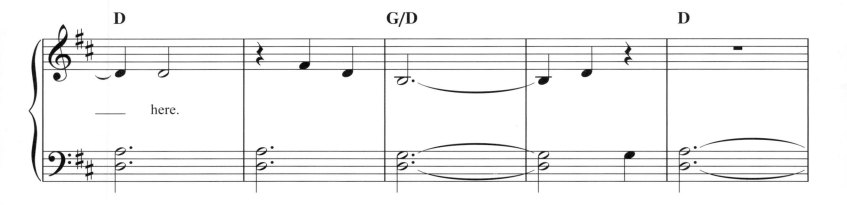

_ here.

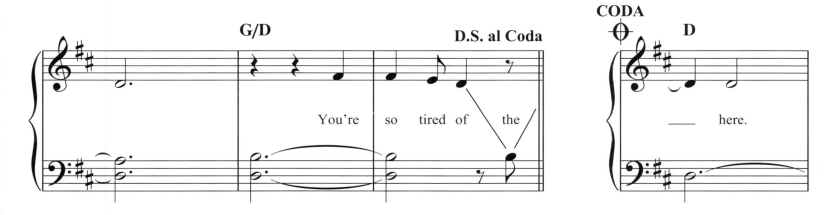

You're so tired of the

_____ here.

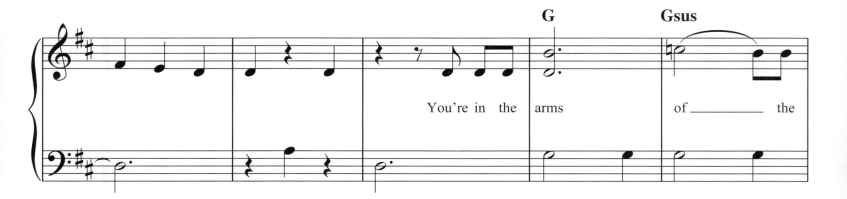

You're in the arms of _____ the

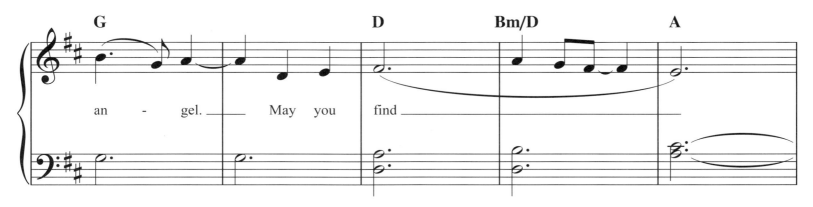

an - gel._____ May you find_____

some com - fort _____ here._____

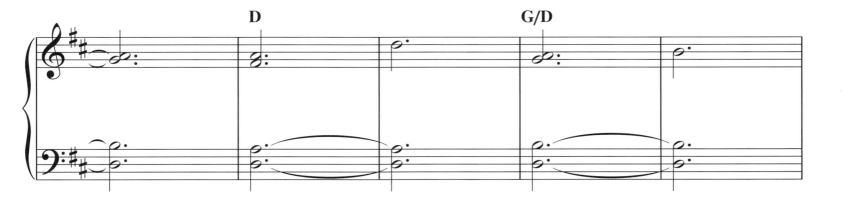

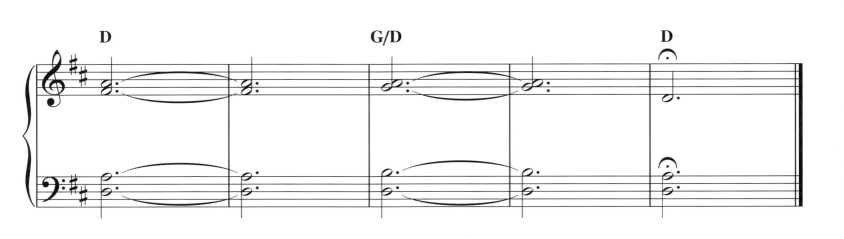

AUTUMN LEAVES

English lyric by JOHNNY MERCER
French lyric by JACQUES PREVERT
Music by JOSEPH KOSMA

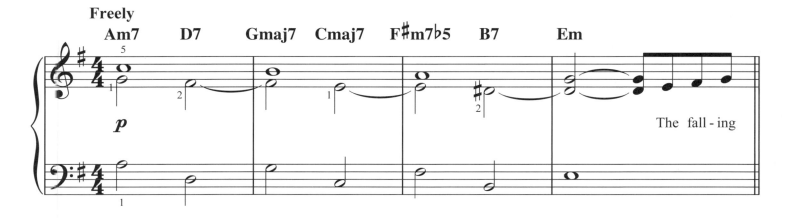

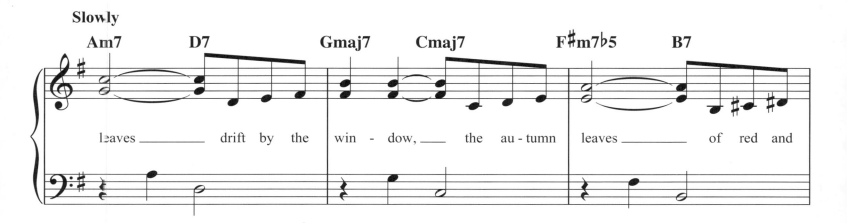

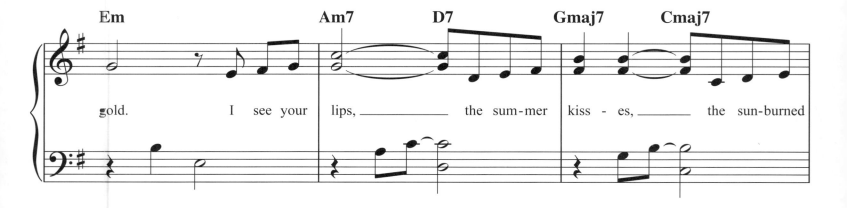

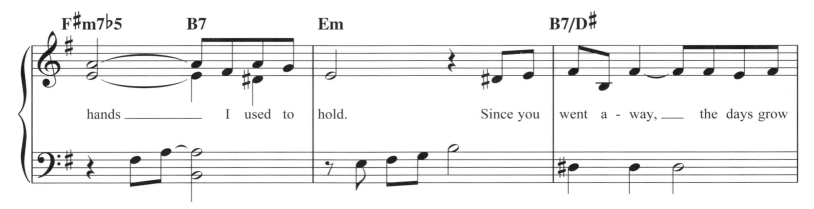

hands _____ I used to hold. Since you went a - way, ___ the days grow

long, _____ and soon I'll hear _____ old win - ter's song. *poco rit.* *a tempo* But I

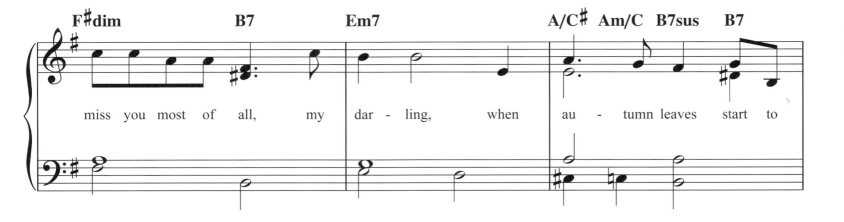

miss you most of all, my dar - ling, when au - tumn leaves start to

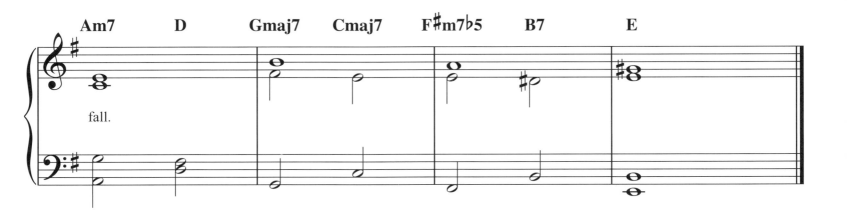

fall.

BAD MOON RISING

Words and Music by
JOHN FOGERTY

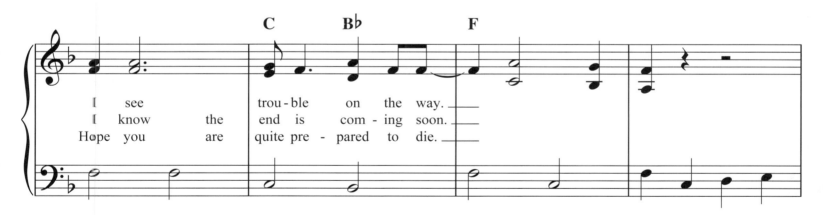

I see the bad __ moon a - ris - ing.
I hear __ hur - ri - canes a - blow - ing.
Hope you __ got your things to - geth - er.

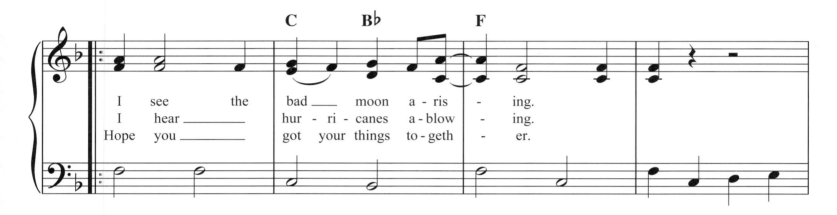

I see trou - ble on the way. __
I know the end is com - ing soon. __
Hope you are quite pre - pared to die. __

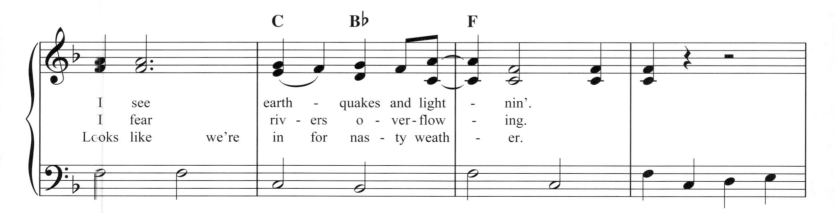

I see earth - quakes and light - nin'.
I fear riv - ers o - ver - flow - ing.
Looks like we're in for nas - ty weath - er.

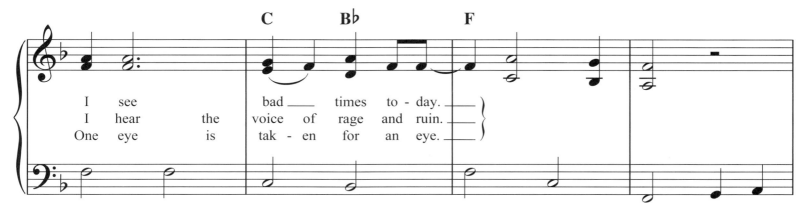

I see the bad____ times to-day.____
I hear the voice of rage and ruin.____
One eye is tak-en for an eye.____

Don't go a-round to-night,____ well, it's bound to take____ your

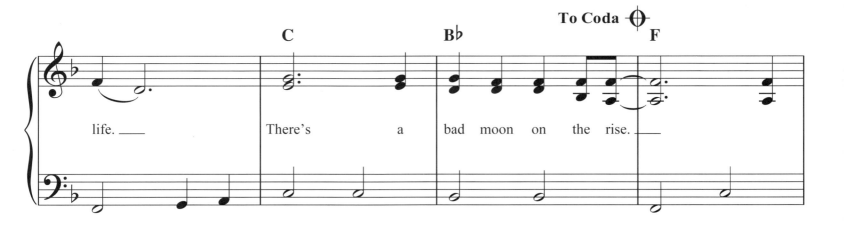

life.____ There's a bad moon on the rise.____

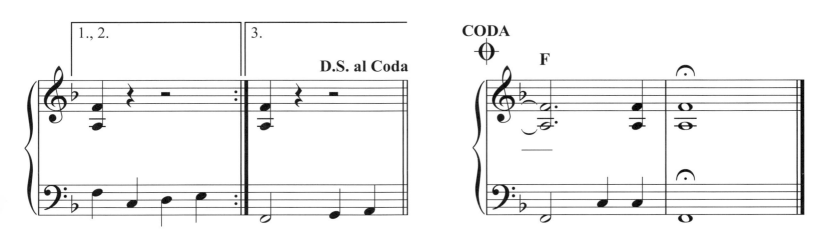

BEN

Words by DON BLACK
Music by WALTER SCHARF

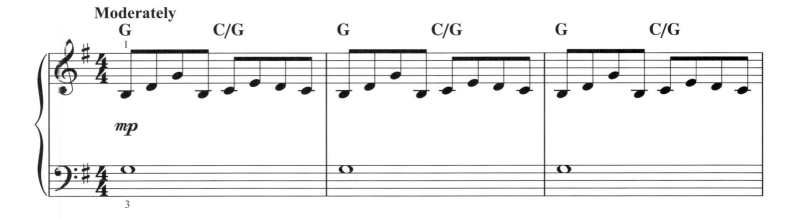

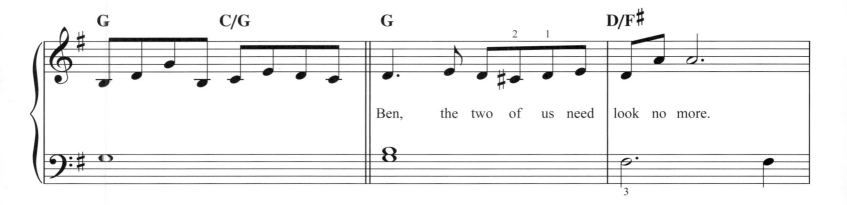

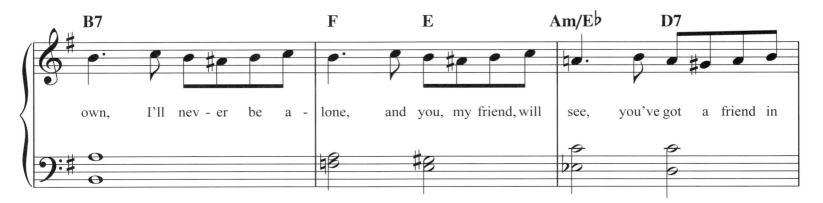

own, I'll nev - er be a - lone, and you, my friend, will see, you've got a friend in

me. _____ Ben, you're al - ways run - ing

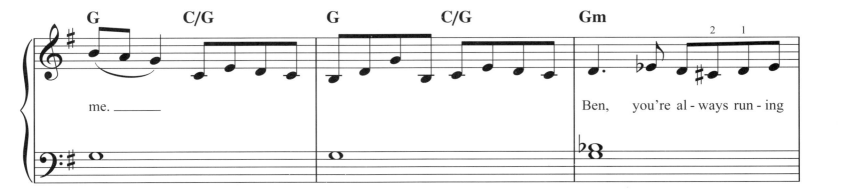

here and there. You feel you're not want - ed an - y - where.

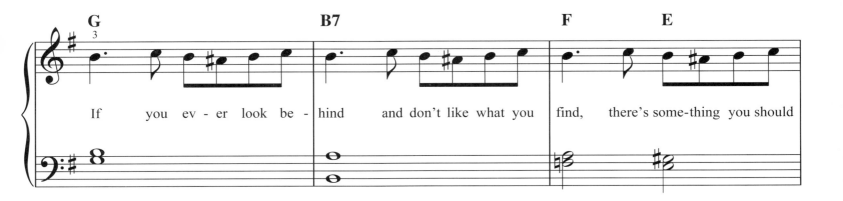

If you ev - er look be - hind and don't like what you find, there's some-thing you should

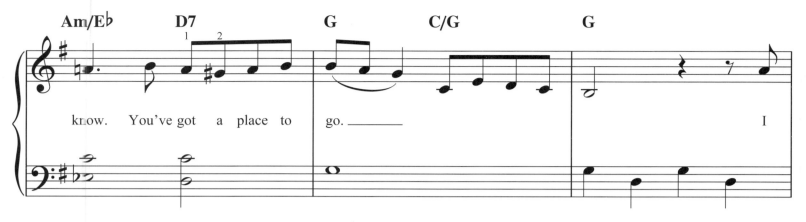

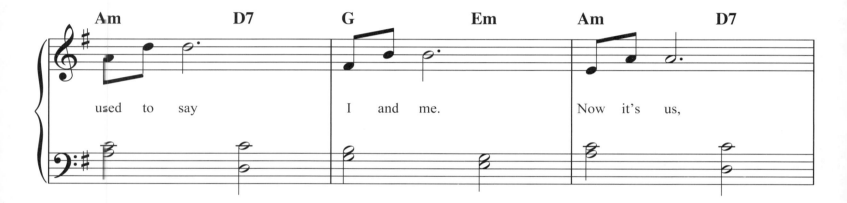

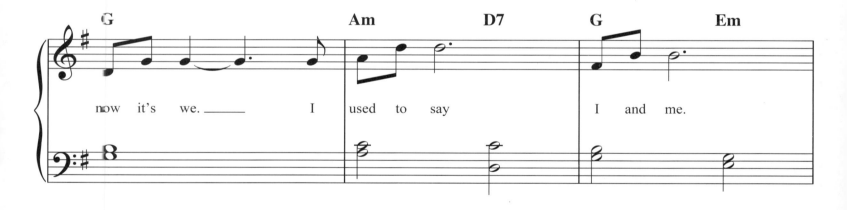

you a - way. I don't lis - ten to a word they say.

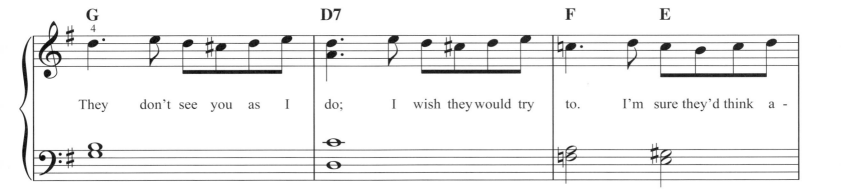

They don't see you as I do; I wish they would try to. I'm sure they'd think a -

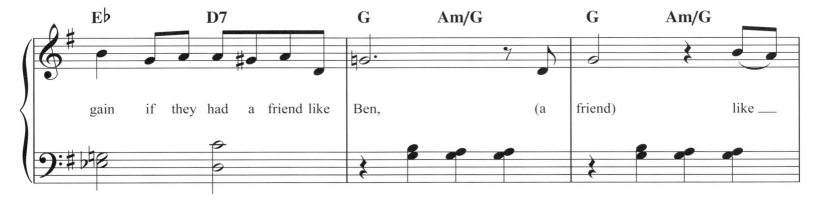

gain if they had a friend like Ben, (a friend) like

Ben, (like Ben) like Ben.

rit.

BLACKBIRD

Words and Music by JOHN LENNON
and PAUL McCARTNEY

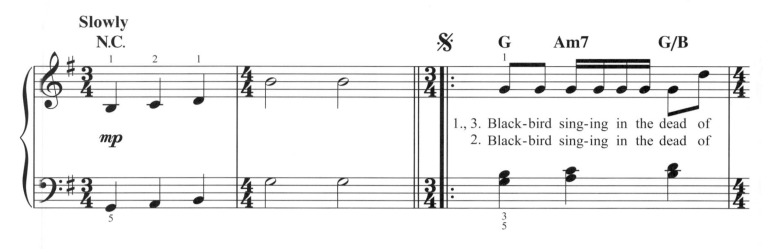

1., 3. Black-bird sing-ing in the dead of
2. Black-bird sing-ing in the dead of

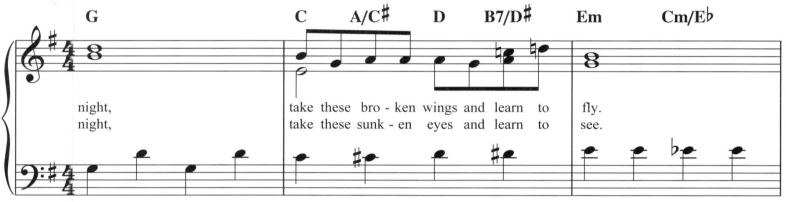

night,   take these bro-ken wings and learn to   fly.
night,   take these sunk-en eyes and learn to   see.

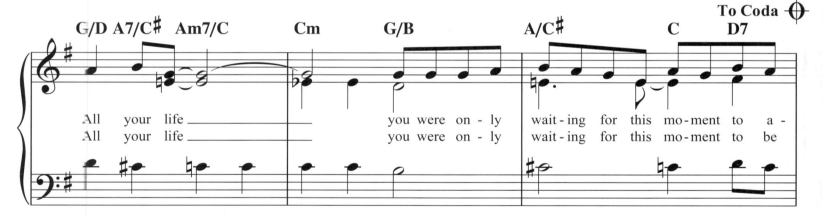

All   your life ___   you were on-ly   wait-ing for this mo-ment to a-
All   your life ___   you were on-ly   wait-ing for this mo-ment to be

rise.

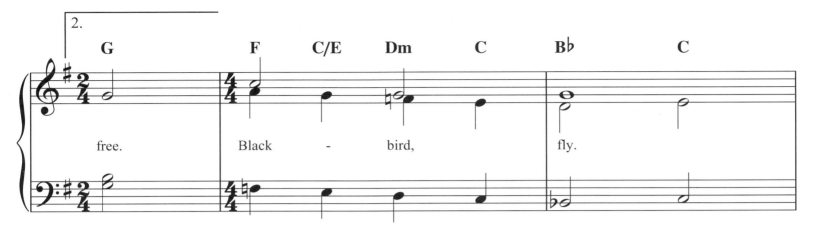

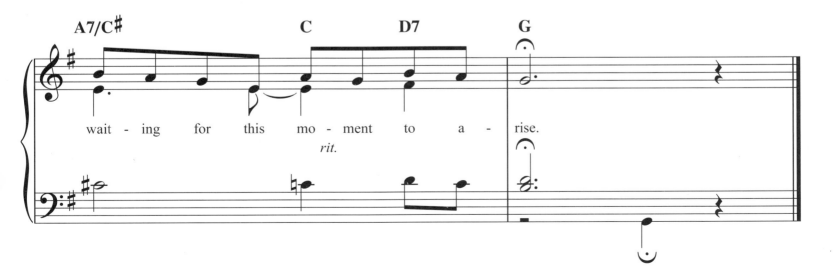

BORN FREE

from the Columbia Pictures' Release BORN FREE

Words by DON BLACK
Music by JOHN BARRY

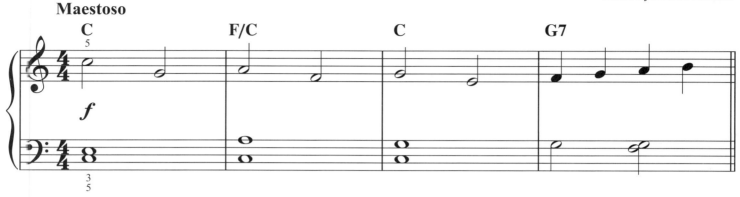

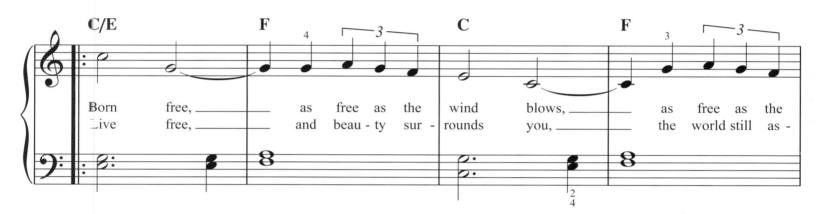

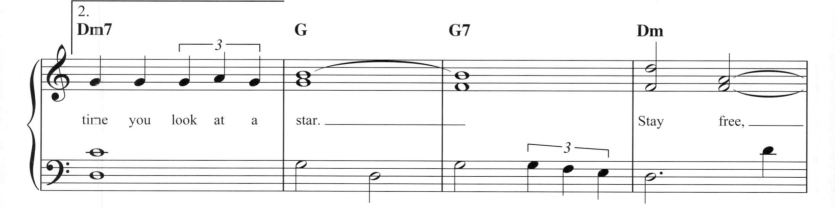

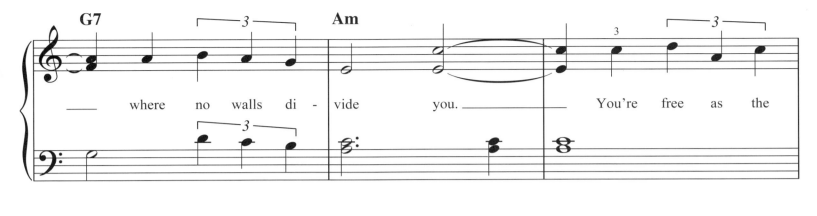

_____ where no walls di - vide you. _____ You're free as the

roar - ing tide, so there's no need to hide.

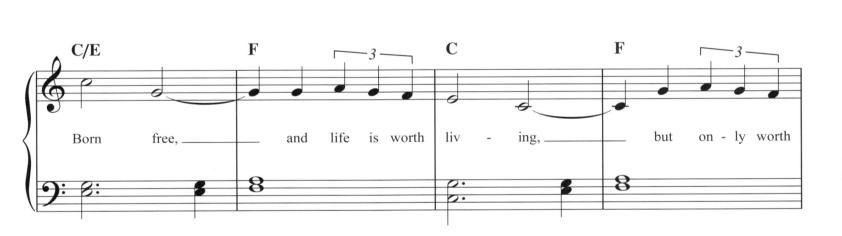

Born free, _____ and life is worth liv - ing, _____ but on - ly worth

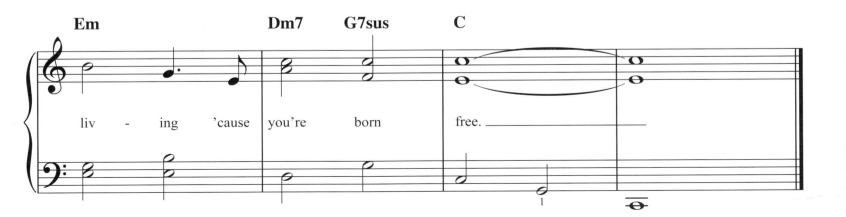

liv - ing 'cause you're born free. _____

BOULEVARD OF BROKEN DREAMS

Words by BILLIE JOE
Music by GREEN DAY

Moderate Rock beat

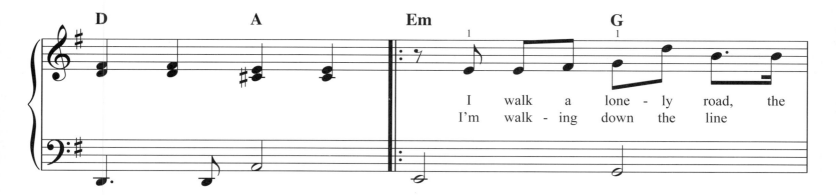

I walk a lone-ly road, the
I'm walk-ing down the line

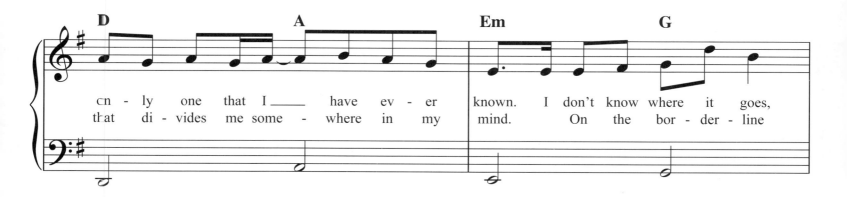

on-ly one that I ___ have ev-er known. I don't know where it goes,
that di-vides me some-where in my mind. On the bor-der-line

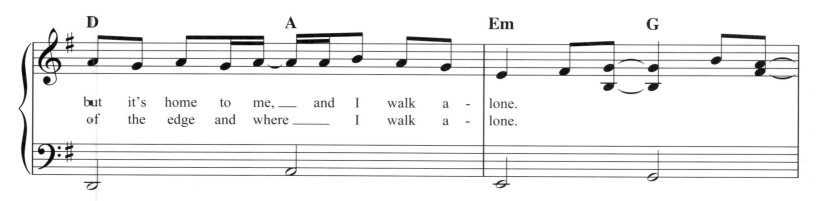

but it's home to me, ___ and I walk a-lone.
of the edge and where ___ I walk a-lone.

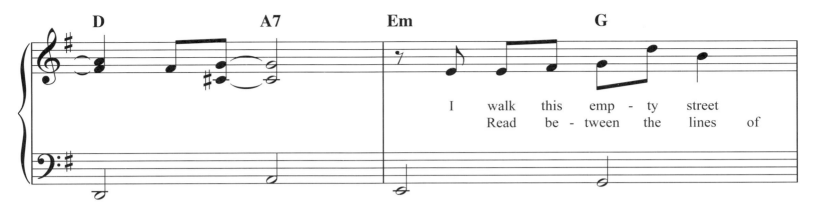

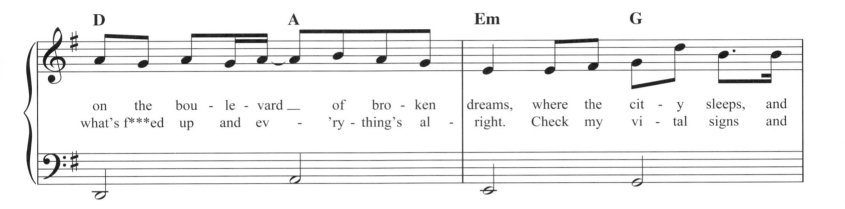

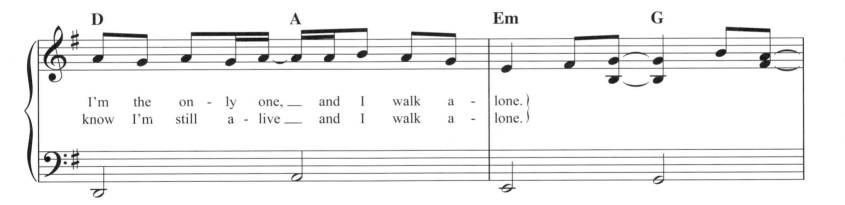

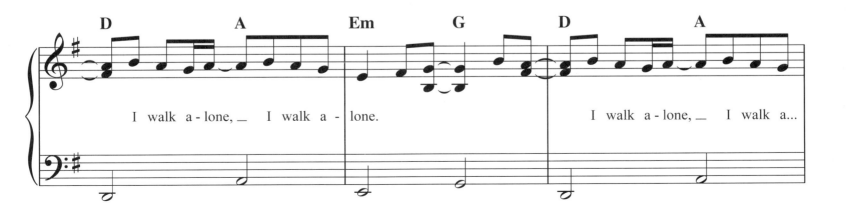

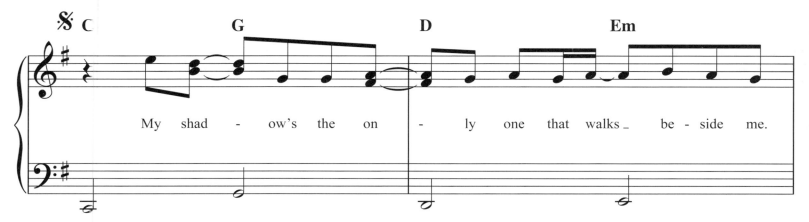

My shad - ow's the on - ly one that walks _ be - side me.

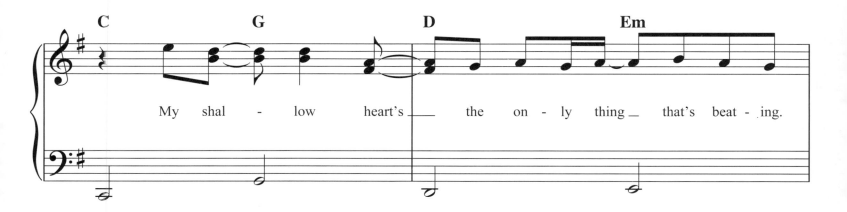

My shal - low heart's _ the on - ly thing _ that's beat - ing.

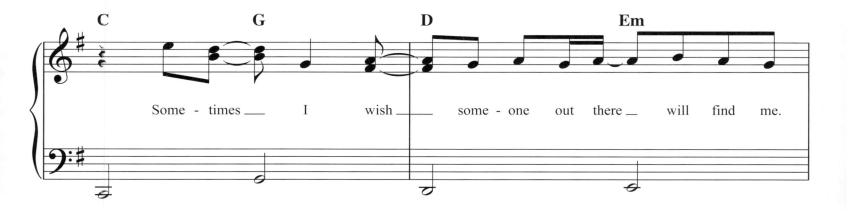

Some - times _ I wish _ some - one out there _ will find me.

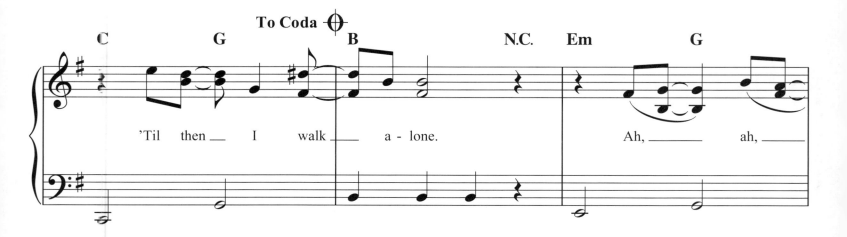

'Til then _ I walk _ a - lone.   Ah, _____ ah, _____

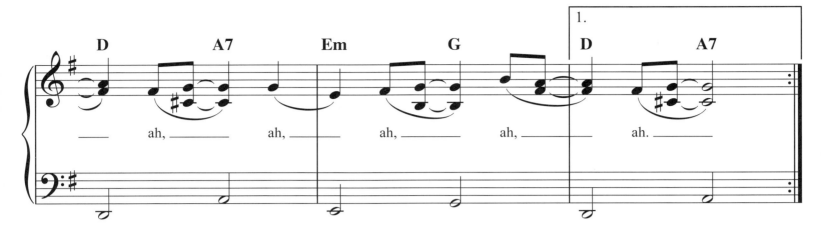

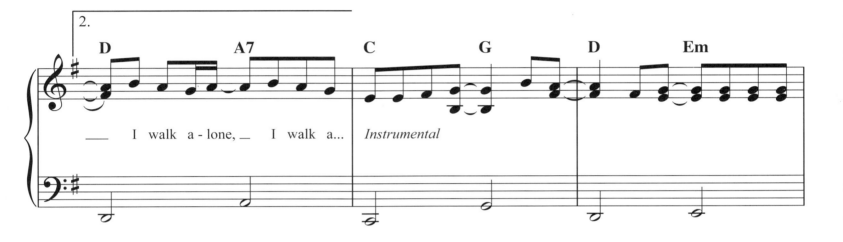

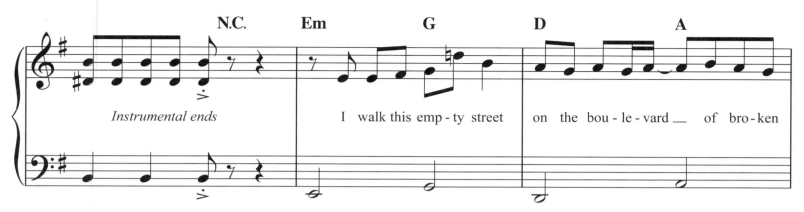

CANDLE IN THE WIND

Words and Music by ELTON JOHN
and BERNIE TAUPIN

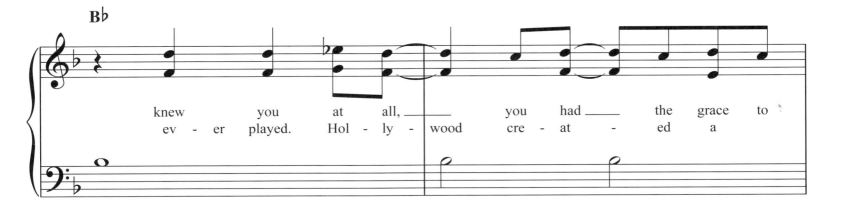

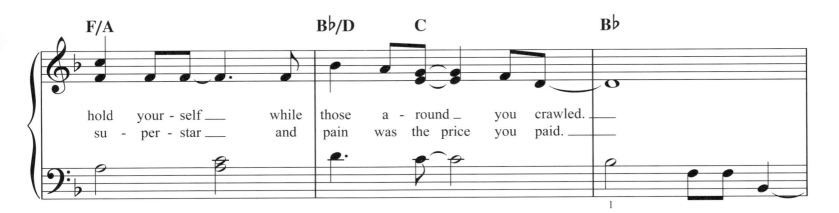

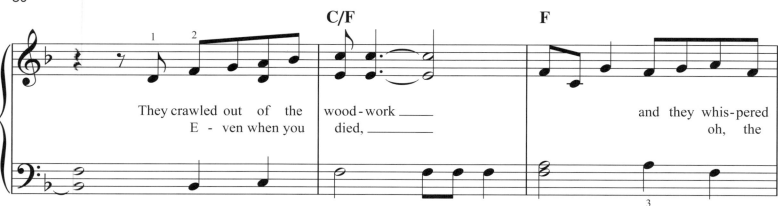

They crawled out of the wood-work _____ and they whis-pered
E - ven when you died, _____ oh, the

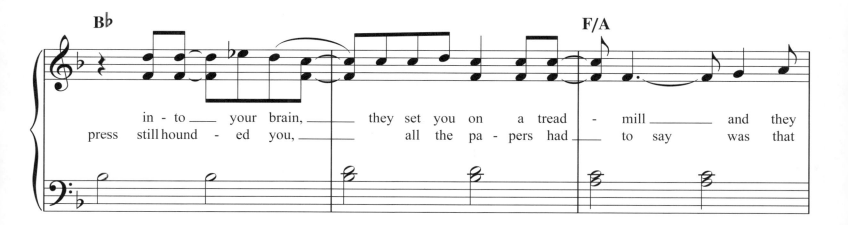

in - to _____ your brain, _____ they set you on a tread - mill _____ and they
press still hound - ed you, _____ all the pa - pers had _____ to say was that

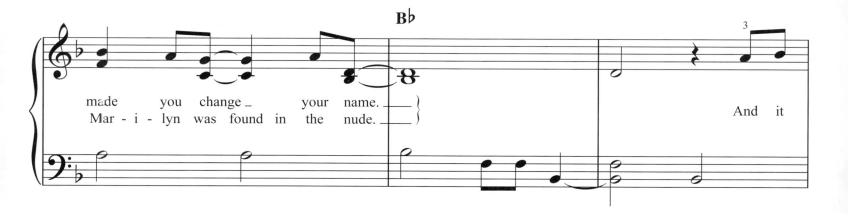

made you change _____ your name. _____
Mar - i - lyn was found in the nude. _____

And it

seems to me you lived your life _____ like a can - dle in _____ the wind. _____

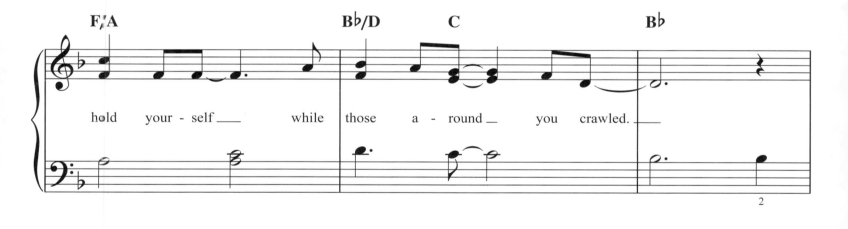

33

twen - ty - sec - ond row ___ who sees you as some-thing more than sex - u - al, ___ more than

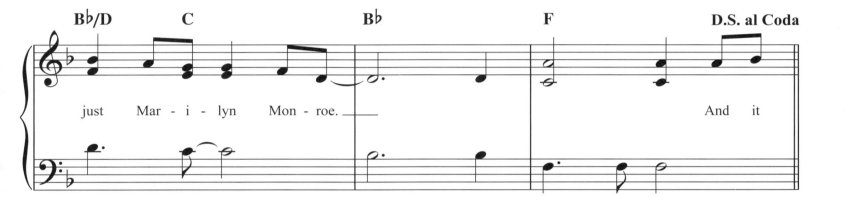

just Mar - i - lyn Mon - roe. ___ And it

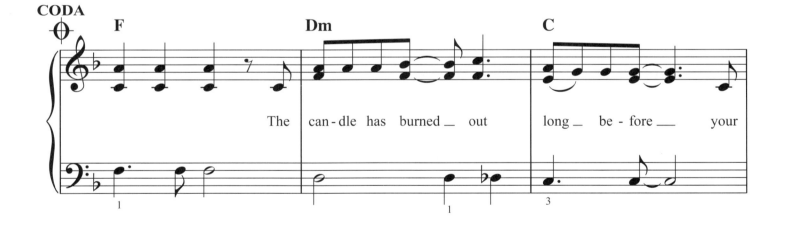

The can-dle has burned ___ out long ___ be - fore ___ your

leg - end ev - er did. ___ *rit.*

CHOPSTICKS

By ARTHUR DE LULLI

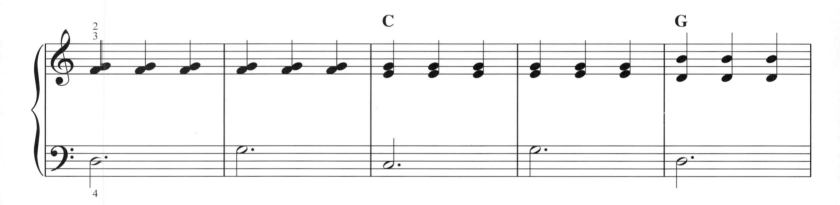

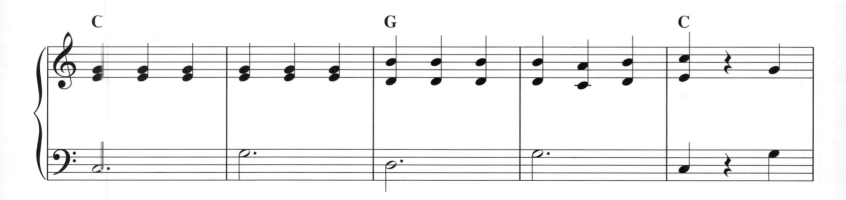

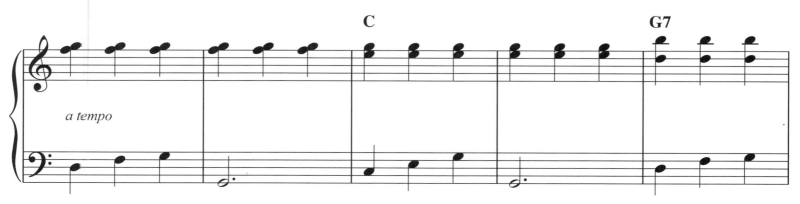

a tempo

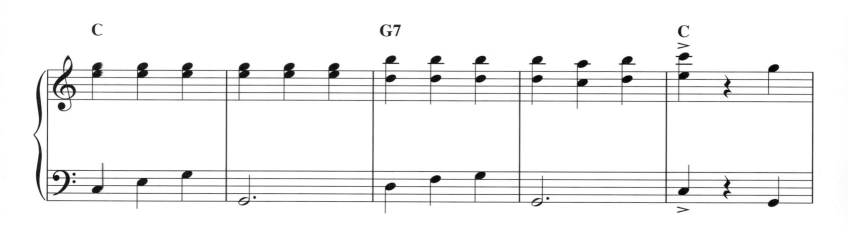

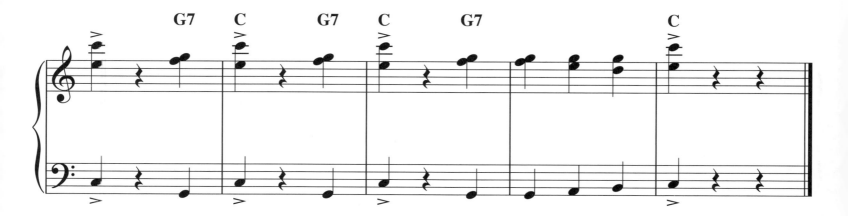

DON'T KNOW WHY

Words and Music by
JESSE HARRIS

I wait-ed till ___ I saw the sun. ___

I don't know why ___ I did-n't come. I left you by ___ the

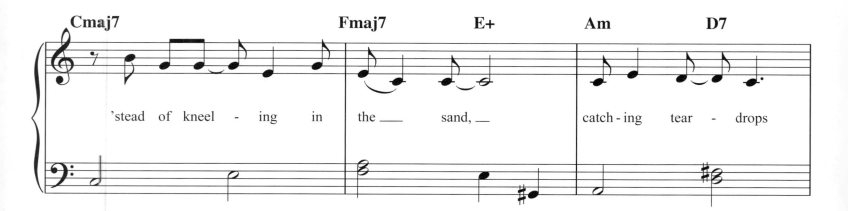

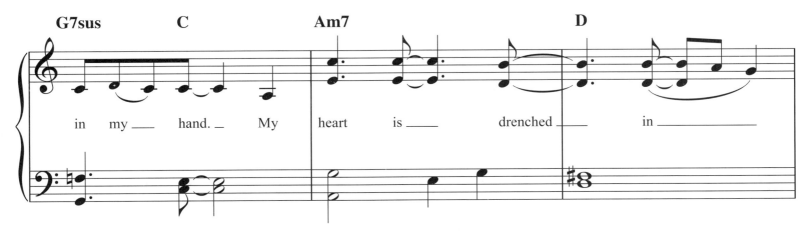

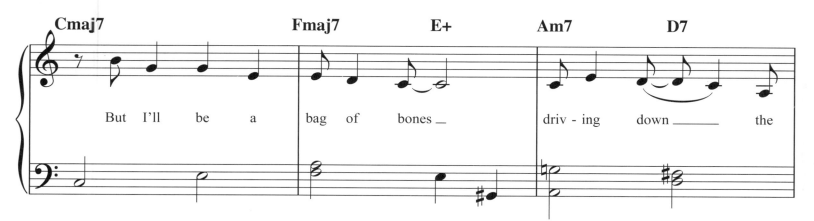

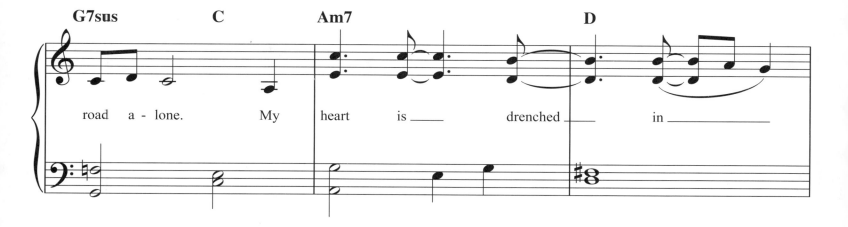

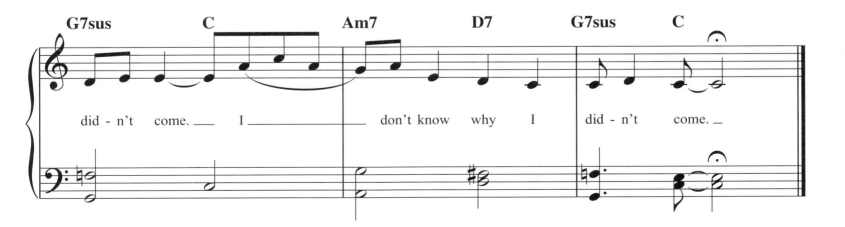

EYE OF THE TIGER
Theme from ROCKY III

Words and Music by FRANK SULLIVAN
and JIM PETERIK

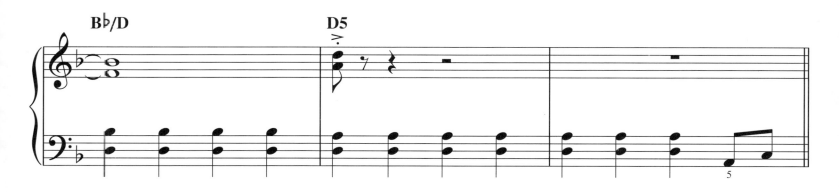

1. Ris - in' up   back on the street, ____ did my time, took my
2. So man - y times it   hap - pens too fast. ____ You trade your pas - sion for
3.-4. *(See additional lyrics)*

chanc - es.   Went the dis - tance. Now I'm   back on my feet, just a
glo - ry.   Don't lose your grip ___ on the   dreams of the past. You must

man and his will to sur - vive.
fight just to keep them a - live. It's the

eye of the ti - ger. It's the thrill of the fight, __ ris - in' up to the chal-lenge of our

To Coda

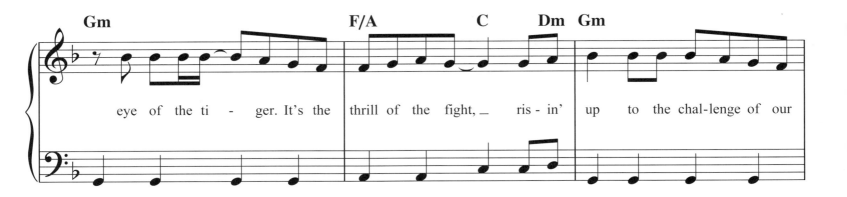

ri - val. And the last known sur-viv - or stalks his prey in the night, __ and he's

D.S. al Coda
(with repeat)

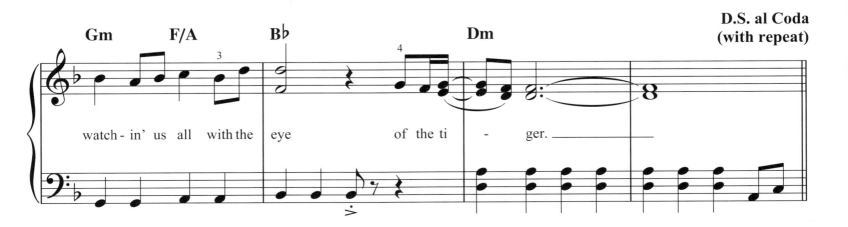

watch - in' us all with the eye of the ti - ger. _____

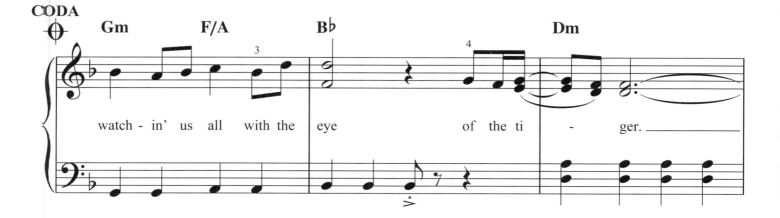

watch - in' us all with the eye of the ti - ger. ____

Additional Lyrics

3. Face to face, out in the heat,
   Hangin' tough, stayin' hungry.
   They stack the odds, still we take to the street
   For the kill with the skill to survive.

4. Risin' up, straight to the top.
   Had the guts, got the glory.
   Went the distance. Now I'm not gonna stop,
   Just a man and his will to survive.

DROPS OF JUPITER
(Tell Me)

Words and Music by PAT MONAHAN,
JIMMY STAFFORD, ROB HOTCHKISS,
CHARLIE COLIN and SCOTT UNDERWOOD

Moderately

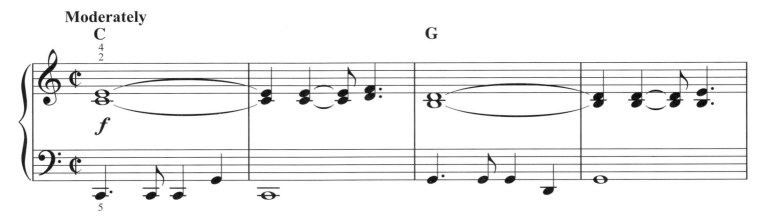

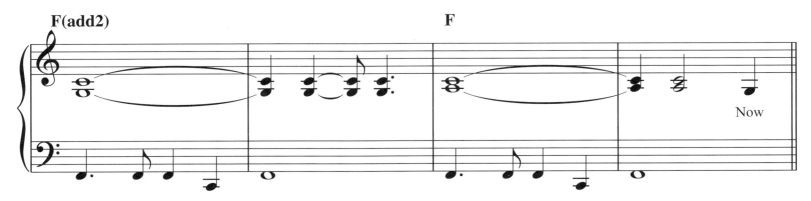

Now

that she's back ___ in the at-mos-phere ___ with drops of Ju-pi-ter
that she's back ___ from that soul va-ca - tion, trac-ing her way ___ through the

in her hair, ___ hey, hey. ___
con-stel - la - tion, ___ hey, ___ hey. ___

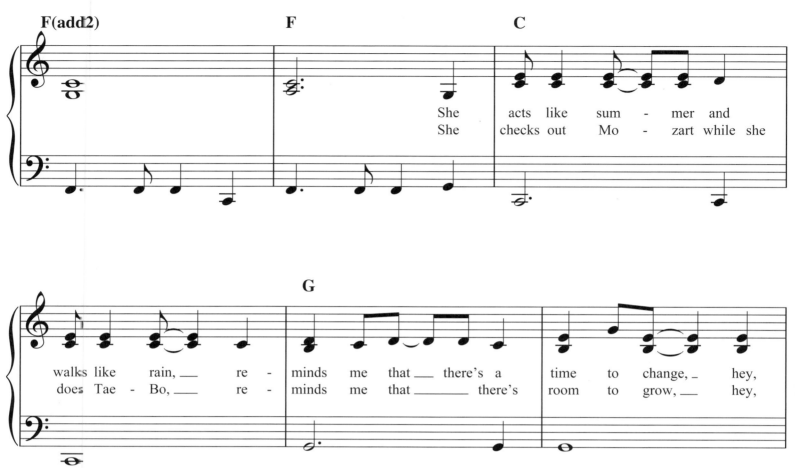

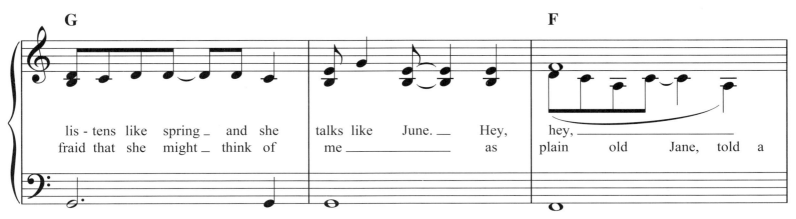

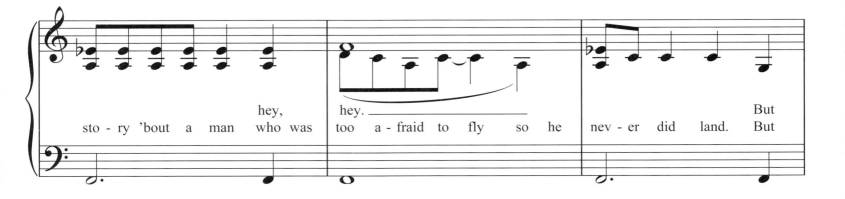

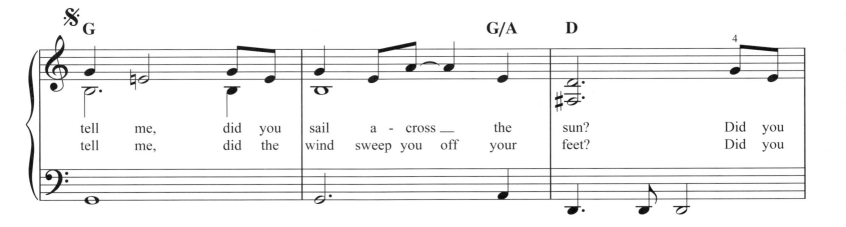

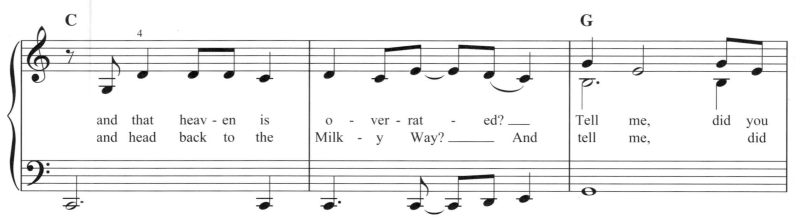

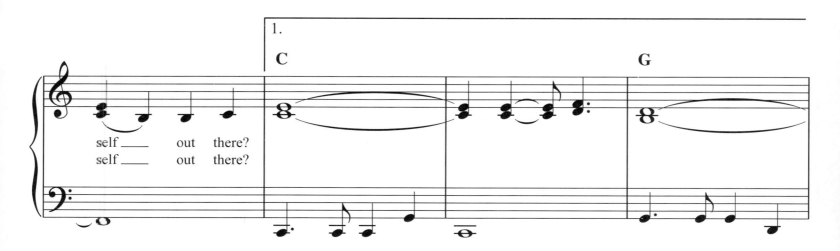

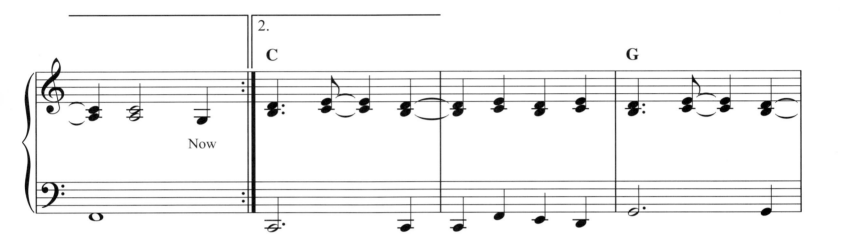

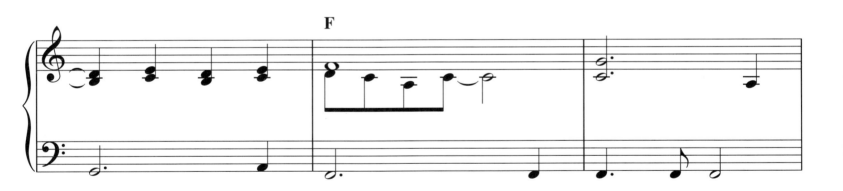

Can you i-mag-ine no love, pride, __ deep-

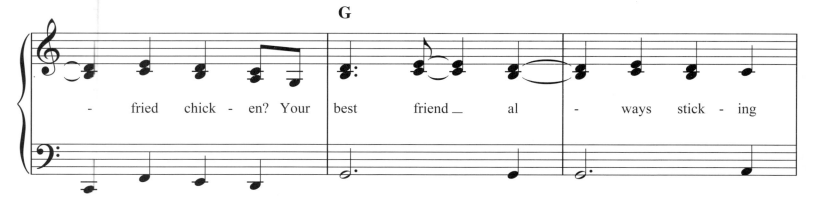

- fried chick - en? Your best friend __ al - ways stick - ing

up for you, _____ e - ven when I know you're wrong? __

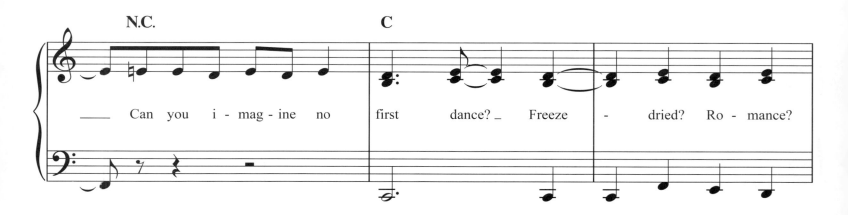

__ Can you i - mag - ine no first dance? __ Freeze - dried? Ro - mance?

Five - hour __ phone con - ver - sa - tion? The best soy lat - te that you

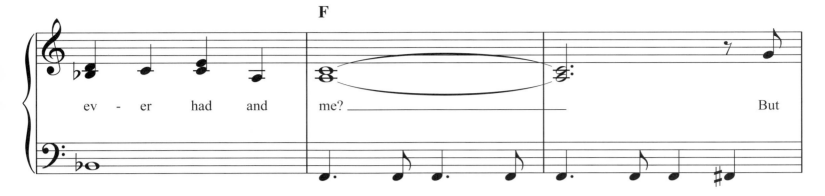

ev - er had and me? _____ But

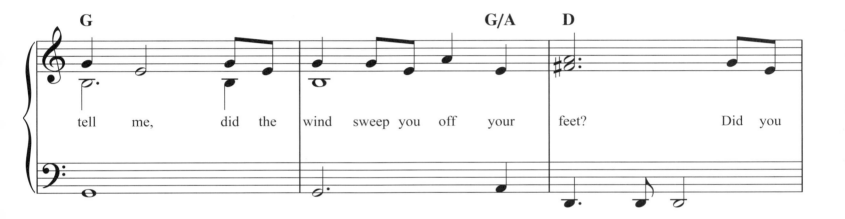

tell me, did the wind sweep you off your feet? Did you

fi - n'lly get the chance to dance a - long ___ the light of

D.S. al Coda
(verse 1)

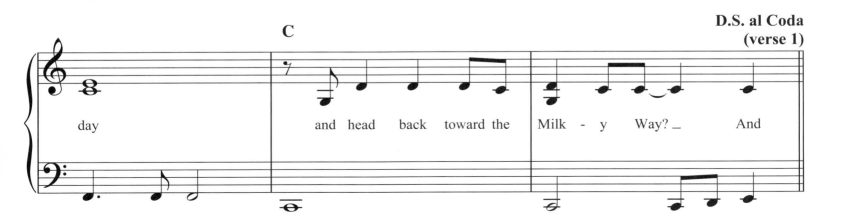

day and head back toward the Milk - y Way? _ And

CODA

look - ing   for ___   your - self?   Na   na ___   na ___

___   na   na   na   na   na ___   na ___   na   na   na

F(add2)

na   na   na   na. ___   And   did   you   fi - n'lly   get   the   chance   to   dance   a - long ___   the   light   of

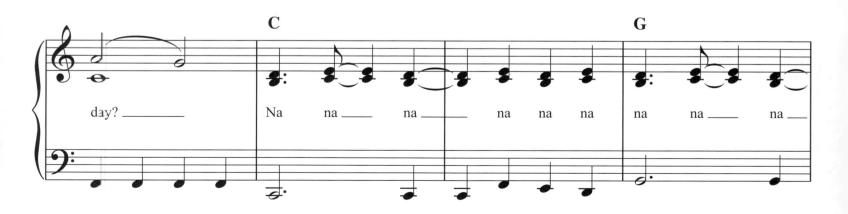

day? ___   Na   na ___   na ___   na   na   na   na   na ___   na ___

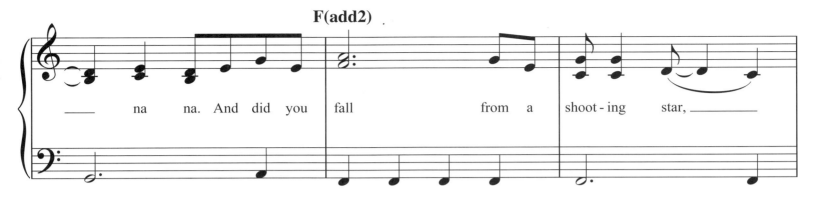

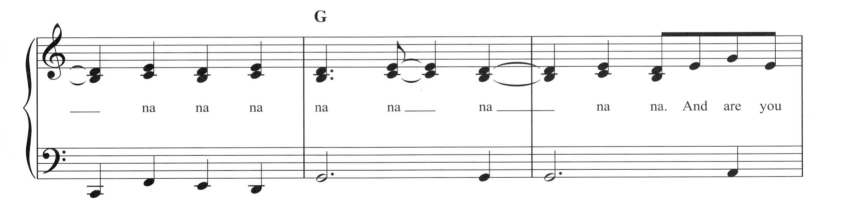

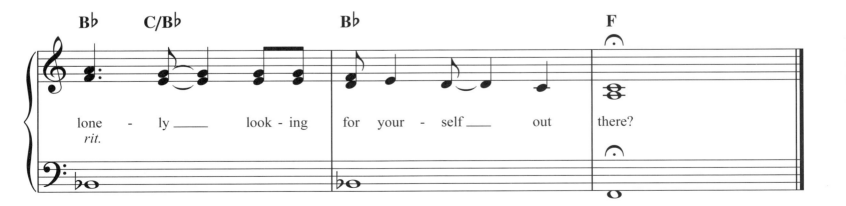

FALLING SLOWLY
from the Motion Picture ONCE

Words and Music by GLEN HANSARD
and MARKETA IRGLOVA

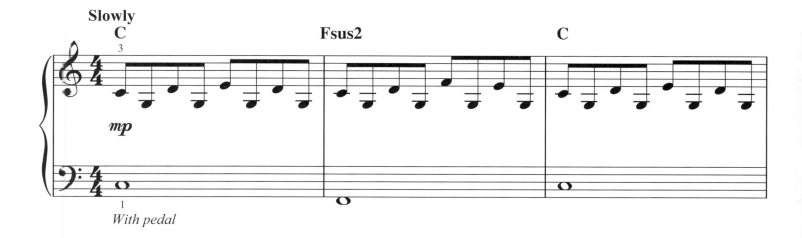

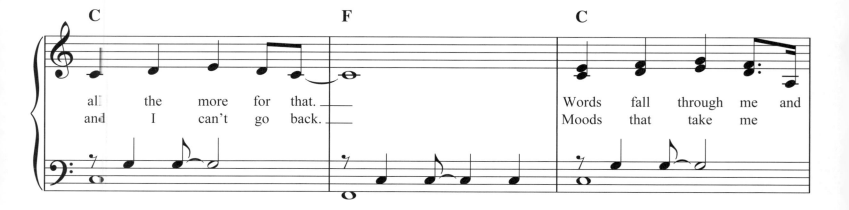

al - ways fool me | and I can't re - act. ___
and e - rase me | and I'm paint - ed black. ___ | Well,

Games that nev - er a - | mount to more than they're | meant will play them-selves
you have suf - fered e - | nough and warred with your - | self. It's time that you

out. ___ | *cresc.* | Take this sink - in'
won. ___

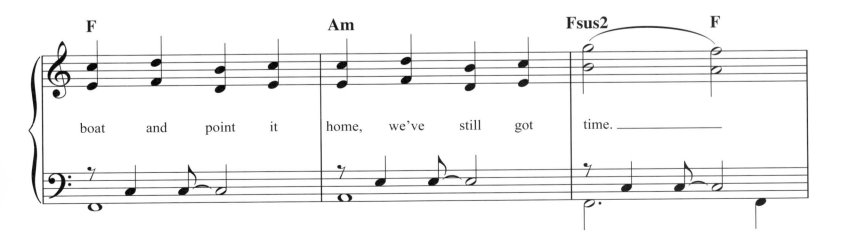

boat and point it | home, we've still got | time. ___

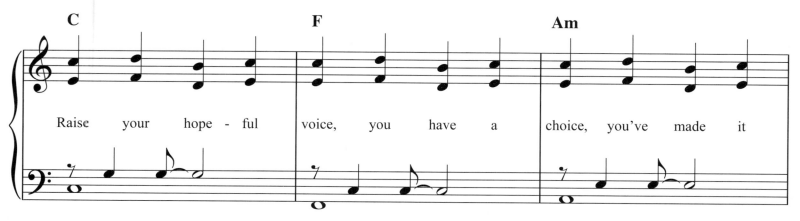

Raise your hope - ful voice, you have a choice, you've made it

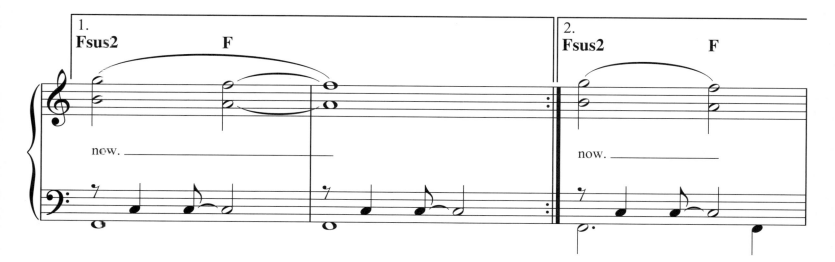

now. _____ now. _____

Fall - ing slow - ly, sing your mel - o - dy, I'll sing it

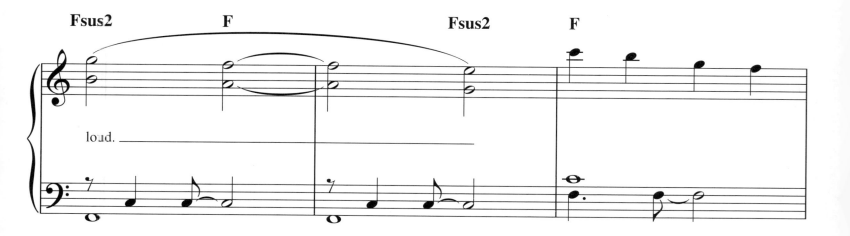

loud. _____

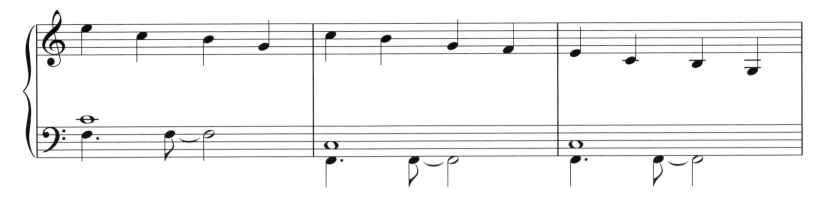

FREE FALLIN'

Words and Music by TOM PETTY
and JEFF LYNNE

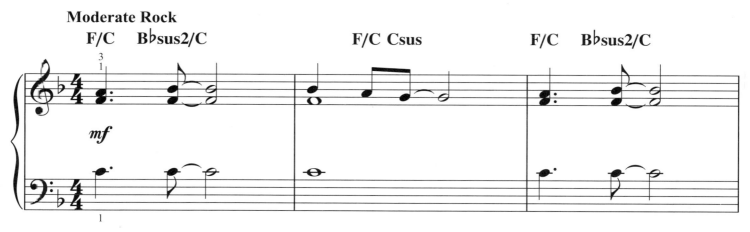

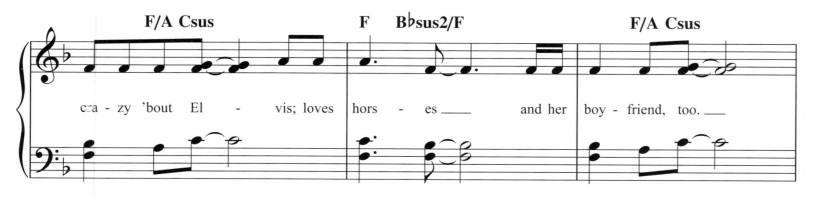

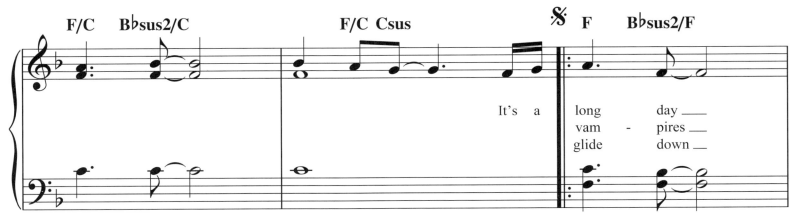

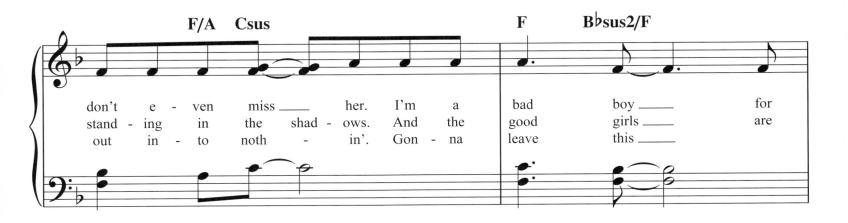

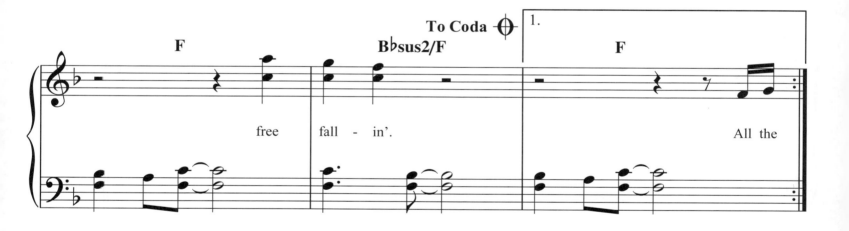

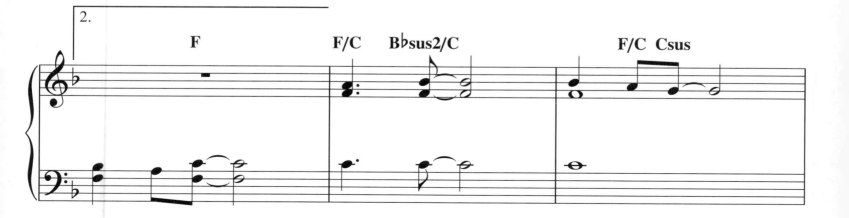

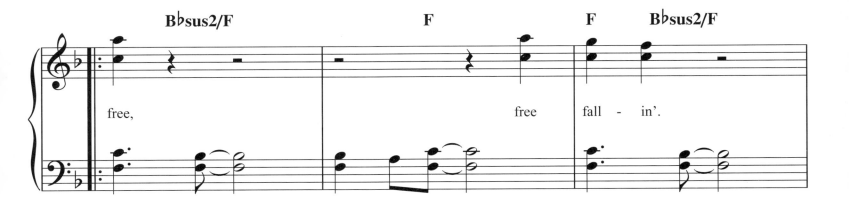

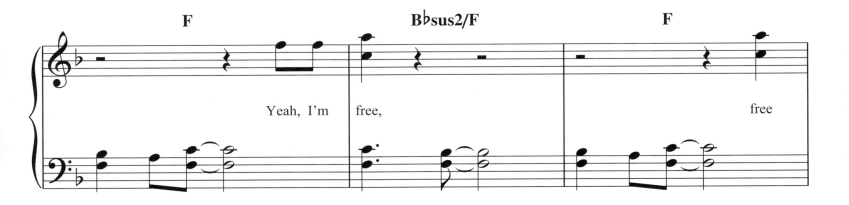

GOLDEN SLUMBERS

Words and Music by JOHN LENNON
and PAUL McCARTNEY

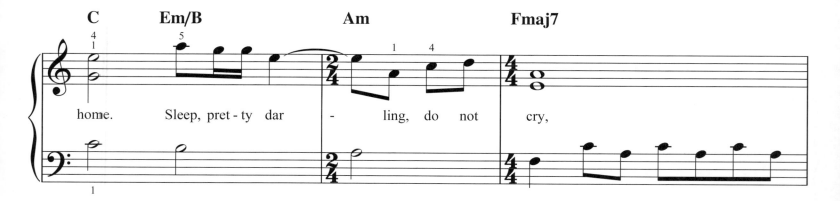

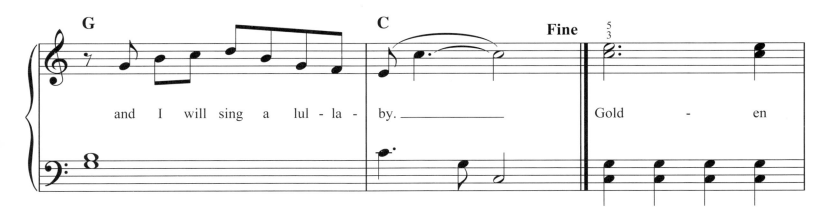

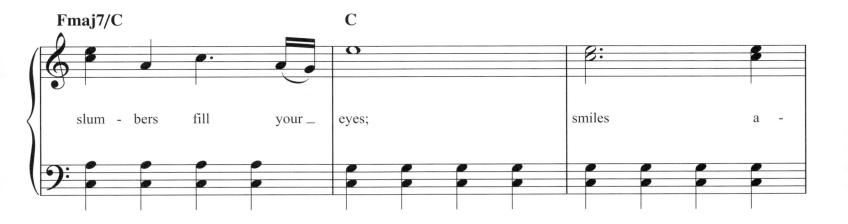

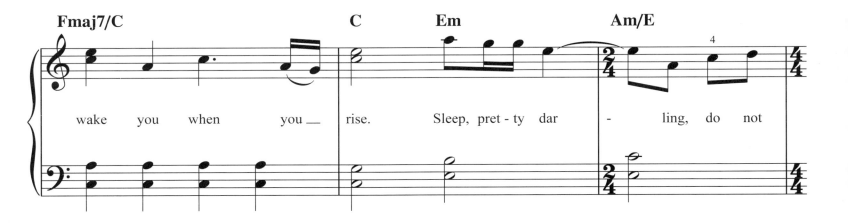

GOOD RIDDANCE
(Time of Your Life)

Words by BILLIE JOE
Music by GREEN DAY

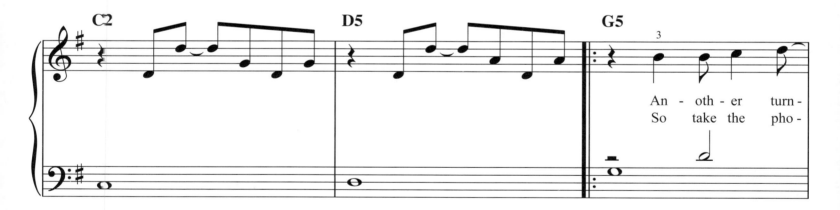

An - oth - er turn -
So take the pho -

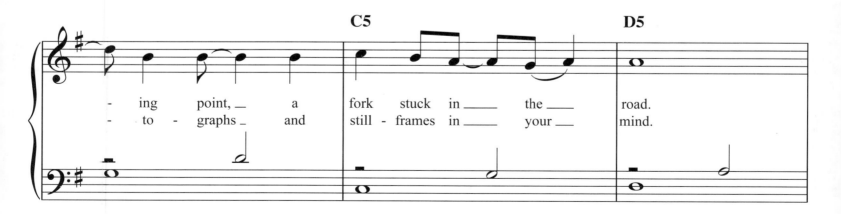

- ing point, a   fork stuck in ___ the ___ road.
- to - graphs ___ and   still - frames in ___ your ___ mind.

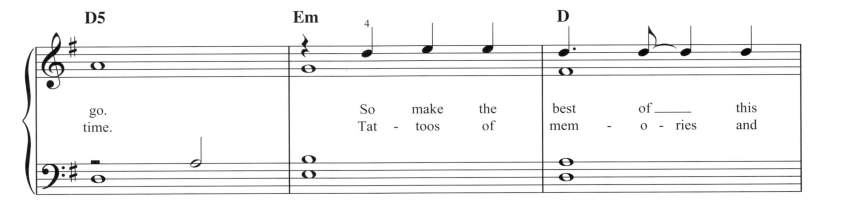

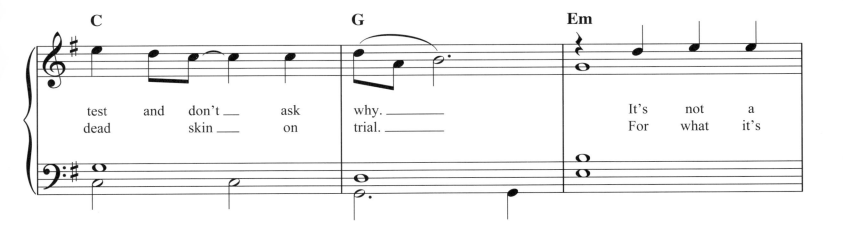

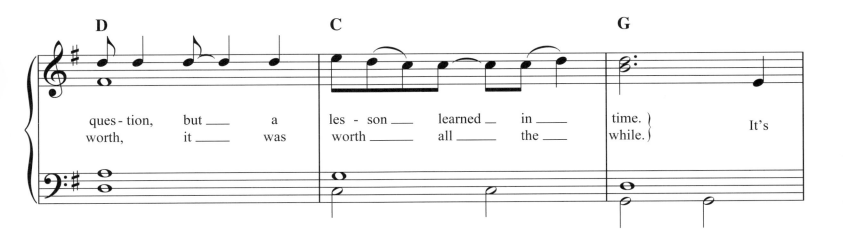

some - thing un - pre - dict - a - ble, ___ but in the end ___ it's

right. I hope you had ___ the time ___ of ___ your

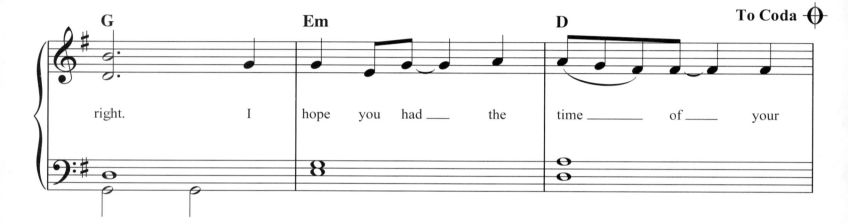

life.

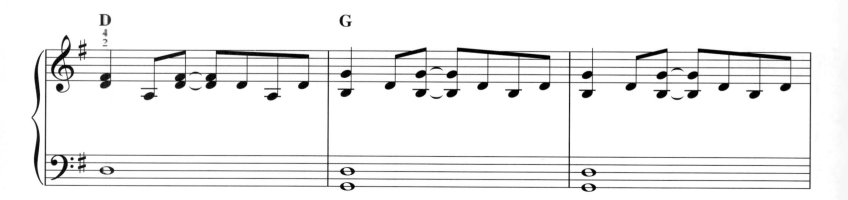

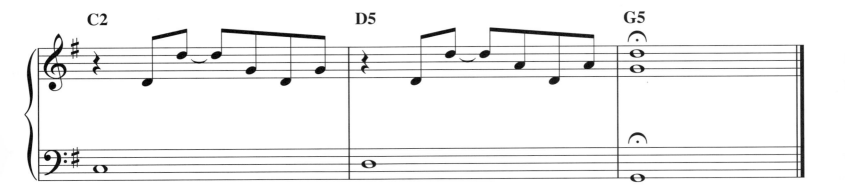

HALLELUJAH

featured in the DreamWorks Motion Picture SHREK

Words and Music by
LEONARD COHEN

Moderately slow, in 2

1. I've

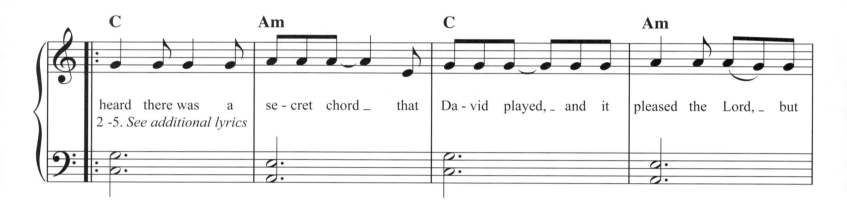

heard there was a | se-cret chord __ that | Da-vid played, __ and it | pleased the Lord, __ but

2 -5. *See additional lyrics*

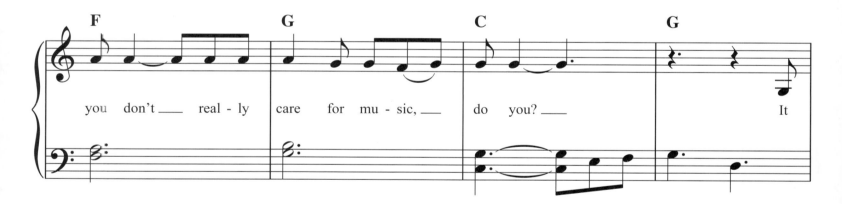

you don't __ real-ly | care for mu-sic, __ | do you? __ | It

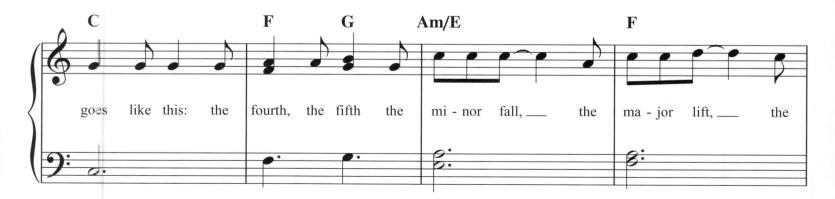

goes like this: the | fourth, the fifth the | mi-nor fall, __ the | ma-jor lift, __ the

baf - fled king ___ com - pos - ing ___ Hal - le - lu - jah. ___ Hal - le -

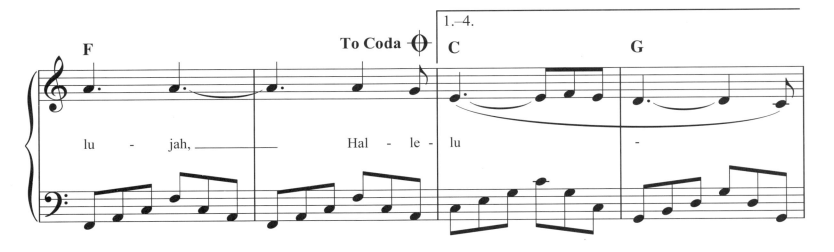

lu - jah, ___ Hal - le - lu - jah, ___ Hal - le -

To Coda | **1.–4.**

lu - jah, ___ Hal - le - lu - -

D.S. al Coda

jah. | 2. Your lu - jah. ___ Hal - le

CODA

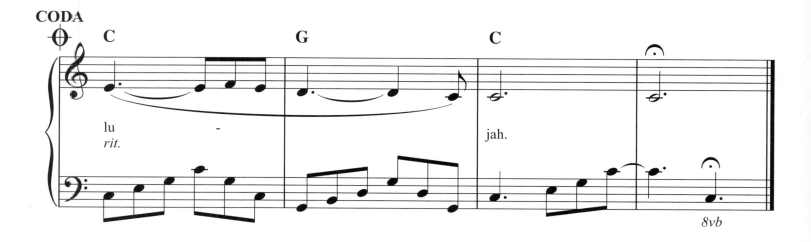

lu
rit.
jah.

8vb

Additional Lyrics

2. Your faith was strong, but you needed proof.
You saw her bathing on the roof.
Her beauty and the moonlight overthrew you.
She tied you to a kitchen chair.
She broke your throne; she cut your hair.
And from your lips she drew the Hallelujah.

3. Maybe I have been here before.
I know this room; I've walked this floor.
I used to live alone before I knew you.
I've seen your flag on the marble arch.
Love is not a victory march.
It's a cold and it's a broken Hallelujah.

4. There was a time you let me know
What's real and going on below.
But now you never show it to me, do you?
And remember when I moved in you,
The holy dark was movin' too,
And every breath we drew was Hallelujah.

5. Maybe there's a God above,
And all I ever learned from love
Was how to shoot at someone who outdrew you.
And it's not a cry you can hear at night.
It's not somebody who's seen the light.
It's a cold and it's a broken Hallelujah.

HAPPY BIRTHDAY TO YOU

Words and Music by MILDRED J. HILL
and PATTY S. HILL

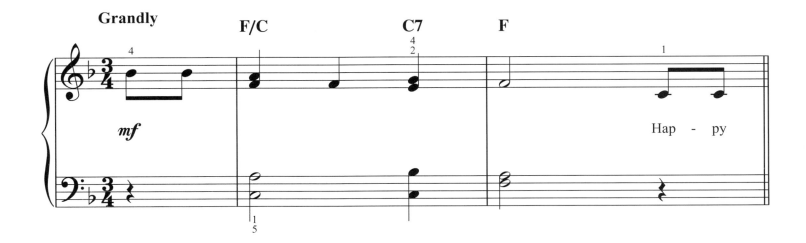

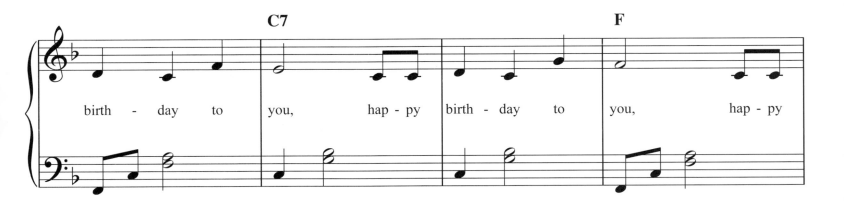

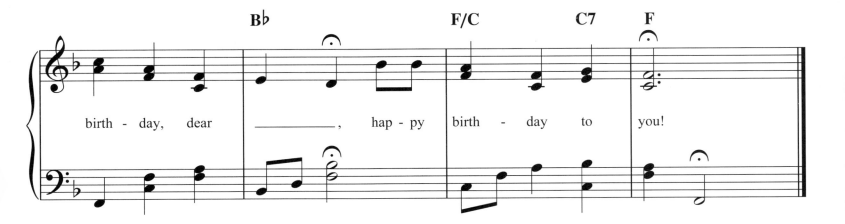

HAPPY
from DESPICABLE ME 2

Words and Music by
PHARRELL WILLIAMS

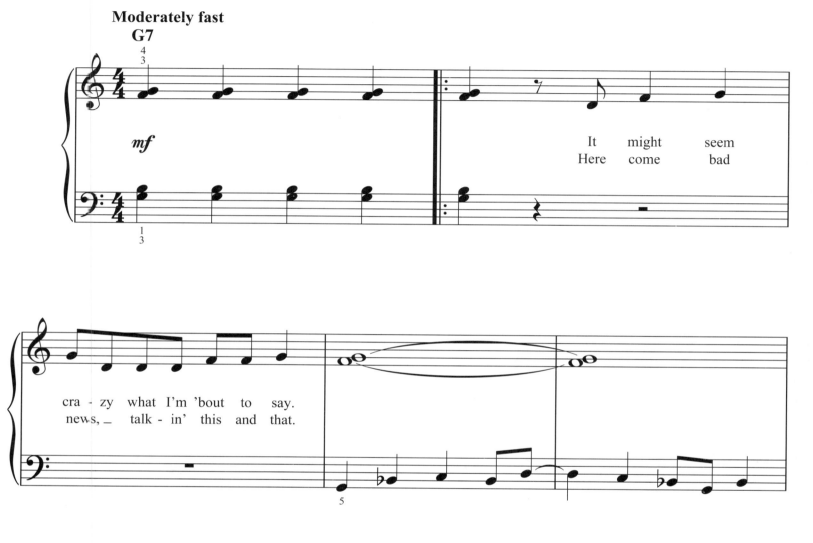

Moderately fast

It might seem
Here come bad

cra - zy what I'm 'bout to say.
news, _ talk - in' this and that.

Sun - shine, _ she's here; you can take a break.
Gim - me all you got, no ___ hold - ing back.

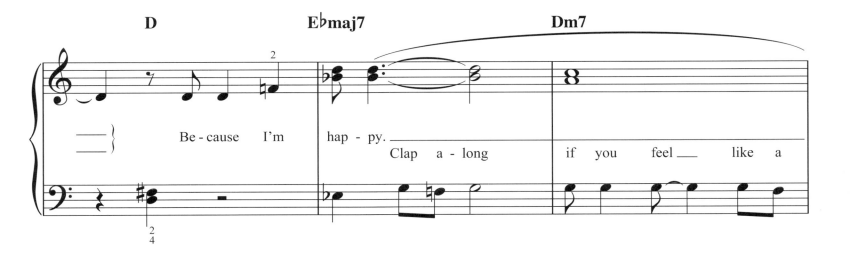

room with - out a roof. Be - cause I'm hap - py. _____ Clap a - long

if you feel ___ like hap - pi - ness is the truth. Be - cause I'm

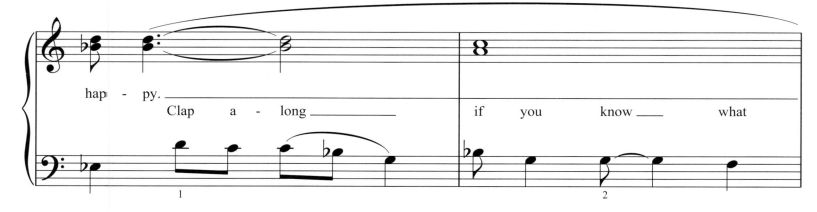

hap - py. _____ Clap a - long _____ if you know ___ what

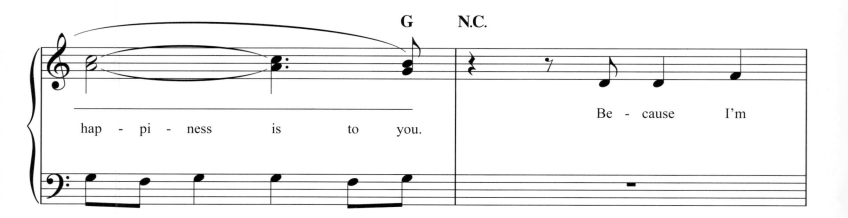

hap - pi - ness is to you. Be - cause I'm

Bring me down, ___ can't noth - in' bring me down; ___ your love is too

high. Bring me down, ___ can't noth - in' bring me down. ___ Be - cause I'm

E♭maj7 **Dm7** **G**

hap - py. ___
Clap a - long if you feel ___ like a room with - out a roof.

4

N.C. **E♭maj7** **Dm7**

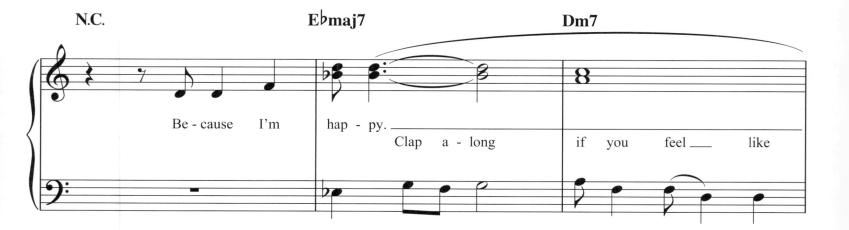

Be - cause I'm hap - py. ___
Clap a - long if you feel ___ like

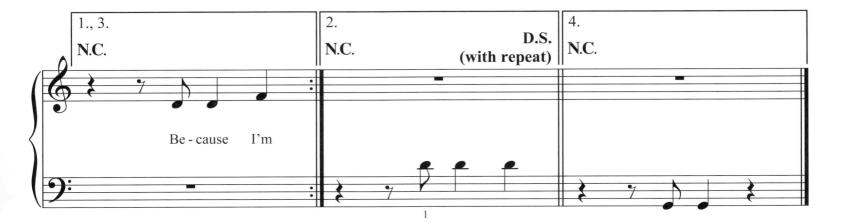

HEART AND SOUL

from the Paramount Short Subject A SONG IS BORN

Words by FRANK LOESSER
Music by HOAGY CARMICHAEL

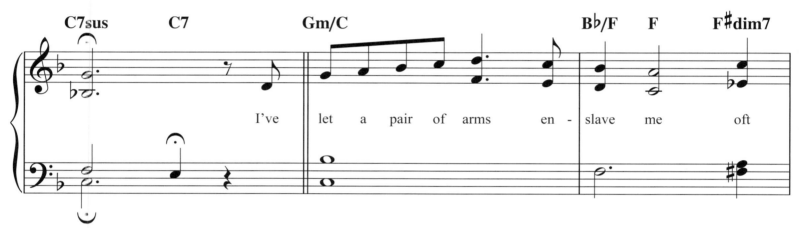

I've let a pair of arms en - slave me oft

times be - fore, but more than just a thrill you

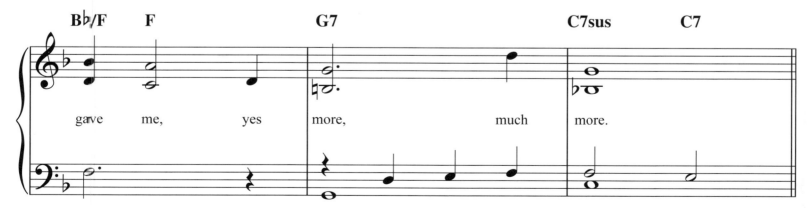

gave me, yes more, much more.

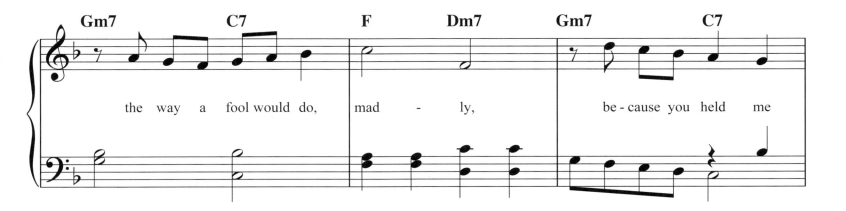

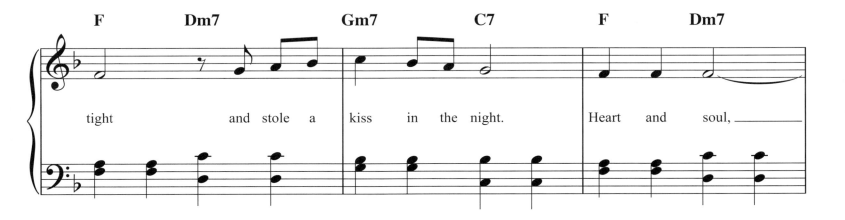

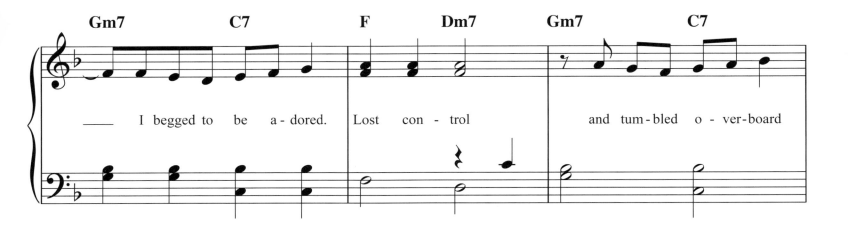

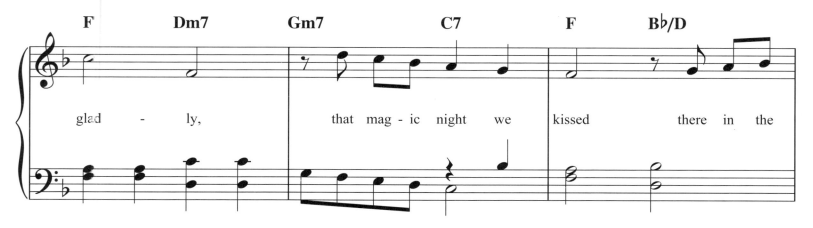

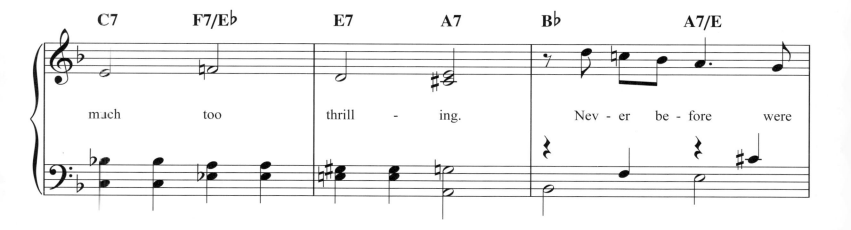

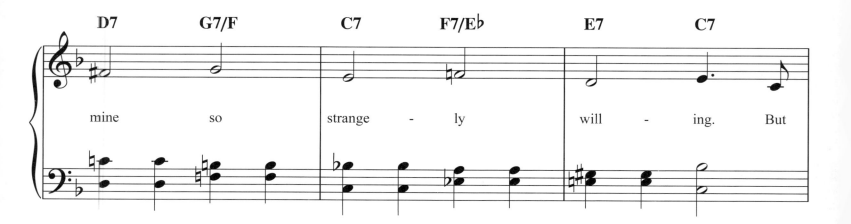

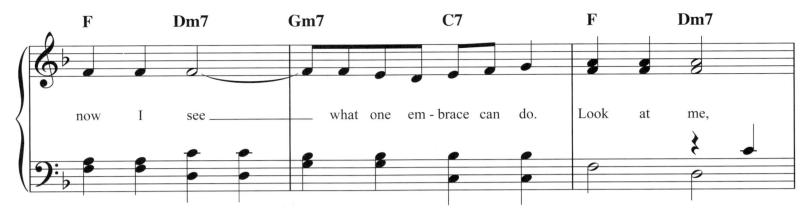

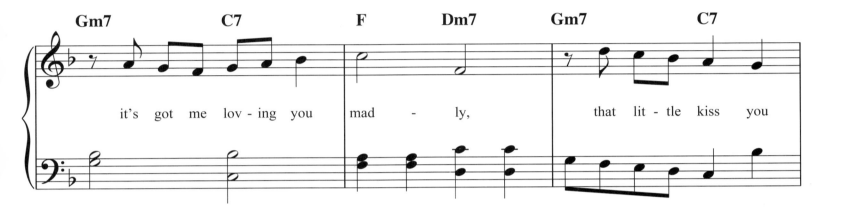

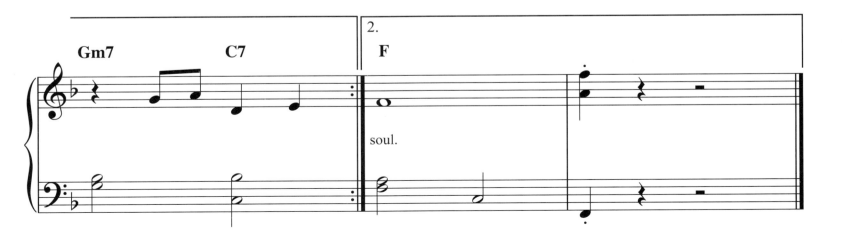

IF YOU LOVE ME REALLY LOVE ME
(Hymne a l'amour)

Words by EDITH PIAF
Music by MARGUERITE MONNOT
English Words by GEOFFREY PARSONS

Slowly and broadly

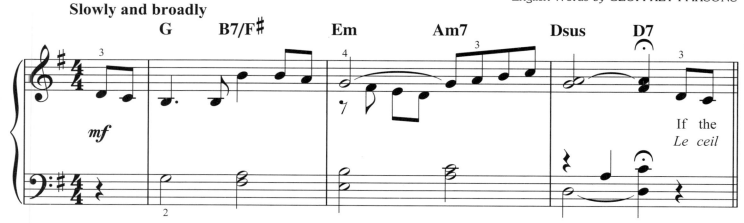

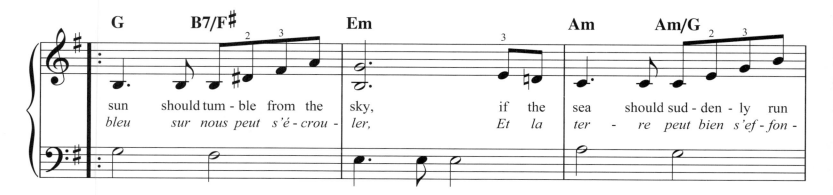

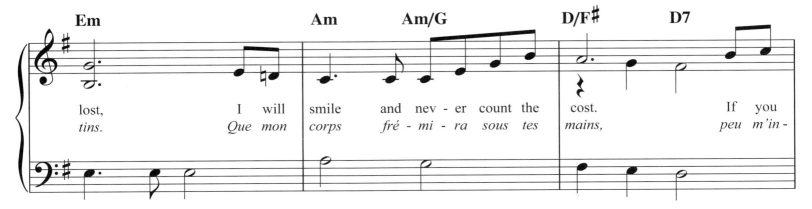

lost,   I will   smile   and   nev-er   count the   cost.   If   you

tins.   Que mon   corps   fré - mi - ra   sous   tes   mains,   peu m'in-

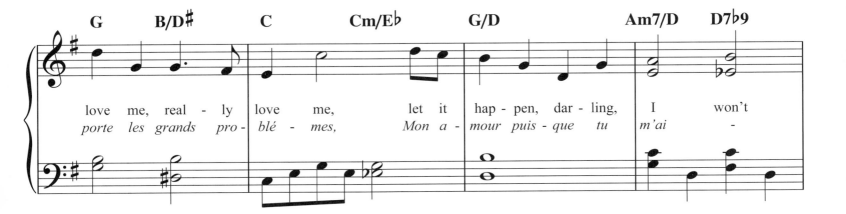

love   me,   real - ly   love   me,   let it   hap - pen,   dar - ling,   I   won't

porte   les   grands   pro - blé - mes,   Mon a - mour   puis - que   tu   m'ai -

A little faster

care.   Shall I   catch a   shoot-ing   star?   Shall I   bring it   where you   are?   If   you

mes.   J'i - rais   jus qu'au   bout   du   monde,   Je me   fe - rais   tein - dre   blonde,   Si   tu

want   me   to,   I will.   You can   set me   an - y   task.   I'll do

me   le   de - mand ais.   On peut   bien   ri - re   de   moi,   Je   fe -

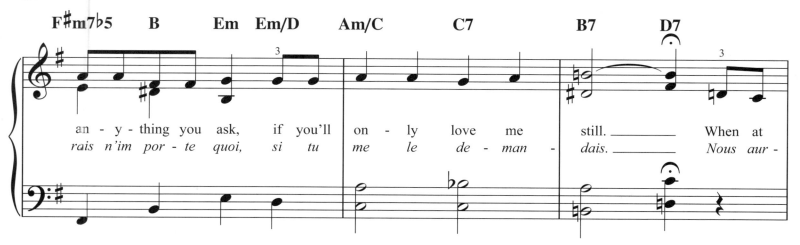

an - y - thing you ask, if you'll on - ly love me still. _____ When at
rais n'im por - te quoi, si tu me le de - man - dais. _____ Nous aur -

Tempo I

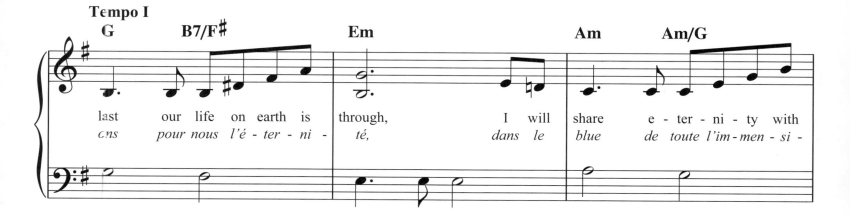

last our life on earth is through, I will share e - ter - ni - ty with
ons pour nous l'é - ter - ni - té, dans le blue de toute l'im - men - si -

you. If you love me, real - ly love me, then what - ev - er hap - pens
té. Dans le ciel plus de pro - blé - mes, dieu ré - u - nit ceux

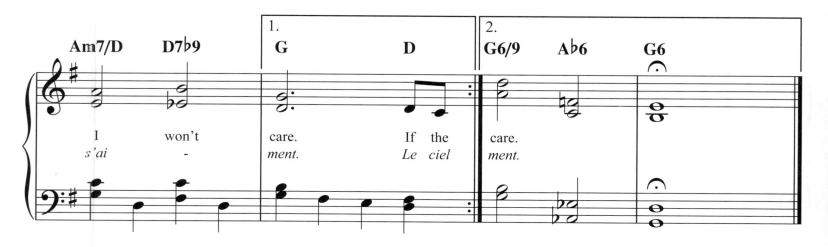

I won't care. If the care.
s'ai - ment. Le ciel ment.

HOME

Words and Music by AMY FOSTER-GILLIES,
MICHAEL BUBLÉ and ALAN CHANG

Moderately slow

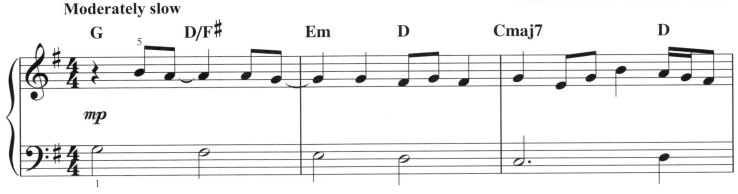

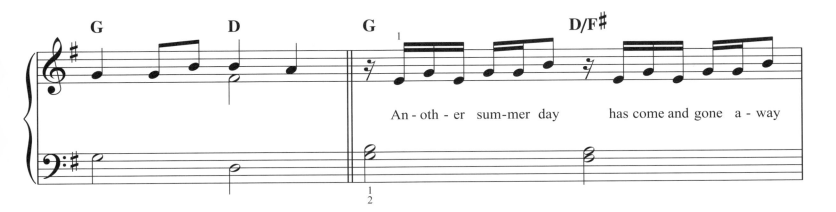

An-oth-er sum-mer day has come and gone a-way

in Par-is and Rome, but I wan-na go home.

May be sur-round-ed by a mil-lion peo-ple; I still feel all a-lone, just wan-na go

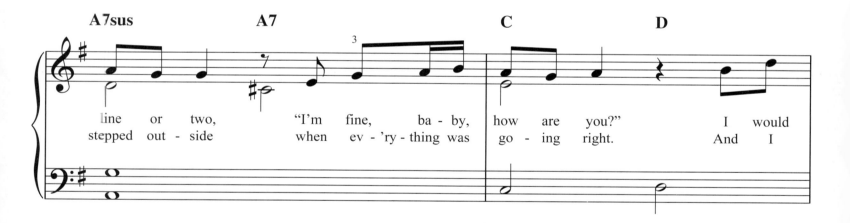

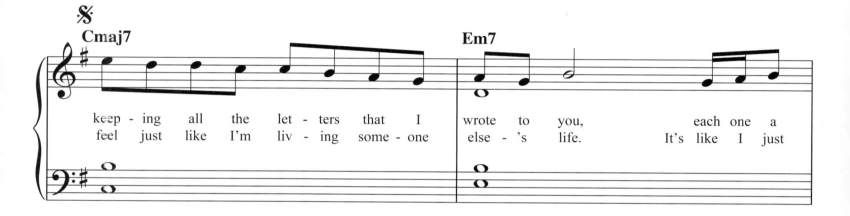

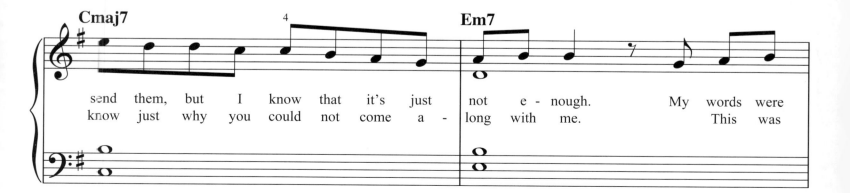

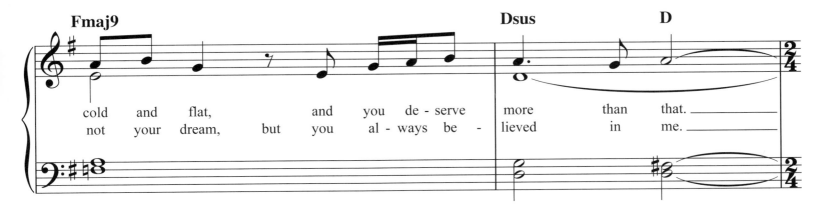

cold and flat, and you de-serve more than that. ____
not your dream, but you al-ways be-lieved in me. ____

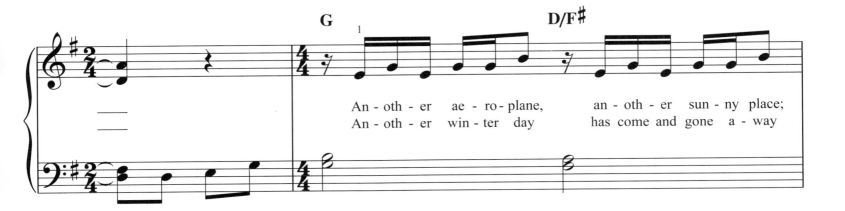

An-oth-er ae-ro-plane, an-oth-er sun-ny place;
An-oth-er win-ter day has come and gone a-way

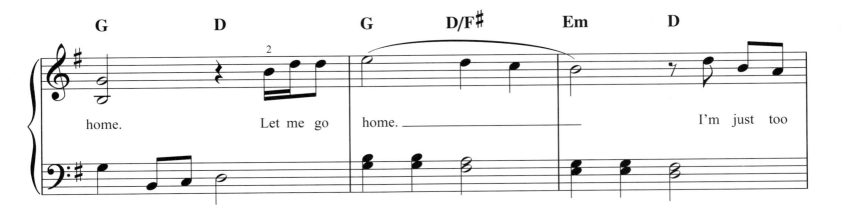

I'm luck-y, I know, but I wan-na go home, ____ I've got to go
in ei-ther Par-is or Rome, and I wan-na go home, ____ let me go

home. Let me go home. ____ I'm just too

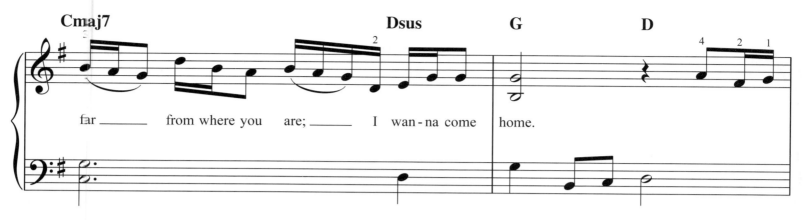

far _____ from where you are; _____ I wan-na come home.

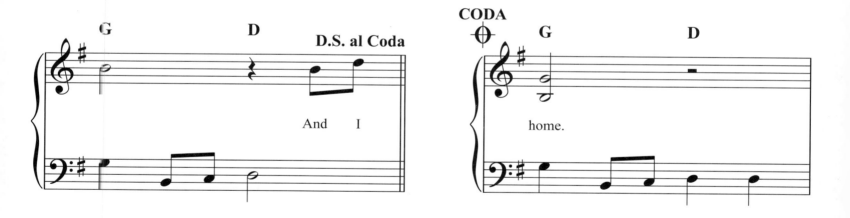

And I

CODA

home.

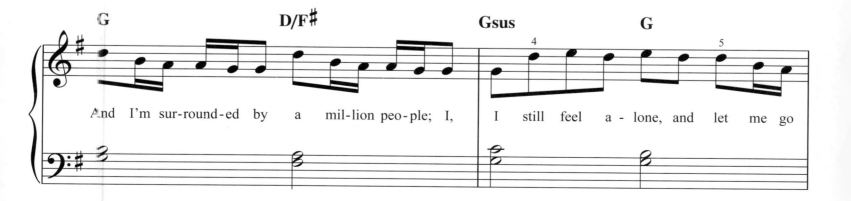

And I'm sur-round-ed by a mil-lion peo-ple; I, I still feel a-lone, and let me go

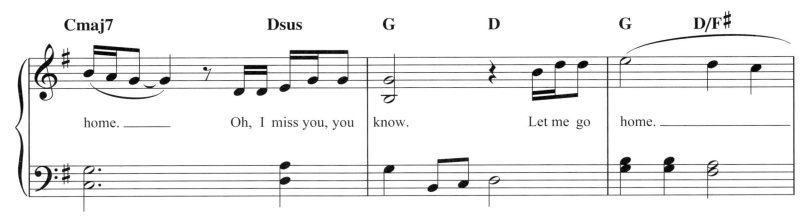

home. _____ Oh, I miss you, you know. Let me go home. _____

_____ I've had my run, and ba-by, I'm done. I've got-ta go home. Let me go

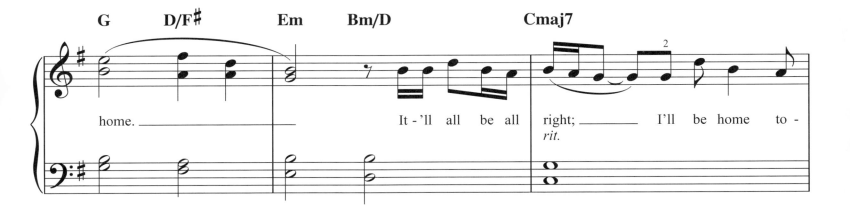

home. _____ It -'ll all be all right; _____ I'll be home to- *rit.*

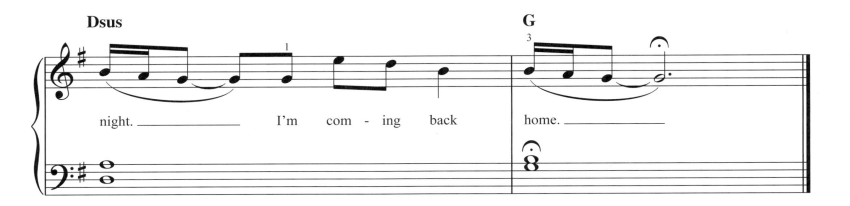

night. _____ I'm com - ing back home. _____

A HORSE WITH NO NAME

Words and Music by
DEWEY BUNNELL

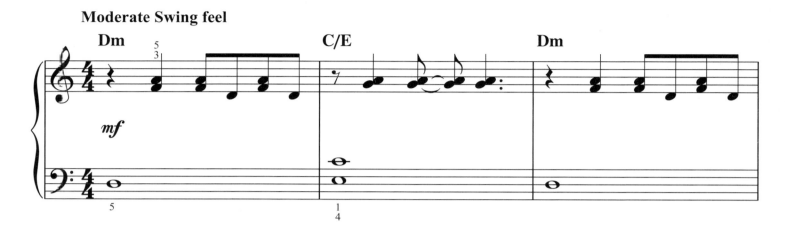

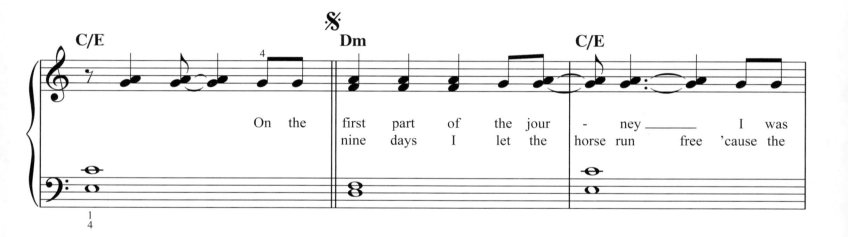

On the first part of the jour- ney _____ I was
nine days I let the horse run free 'cause the

look- ing at all ____ the ____ life. ____
des- ert had turned ____ to ____ sea. ____

There were plants and birds ____ and rocks ____
There were plants and birds ____ and rocks ____

and things,____ there were sand and hills ____ and rings. ____ The
and things,____ there were sand and hills ____ and rings. ____ The

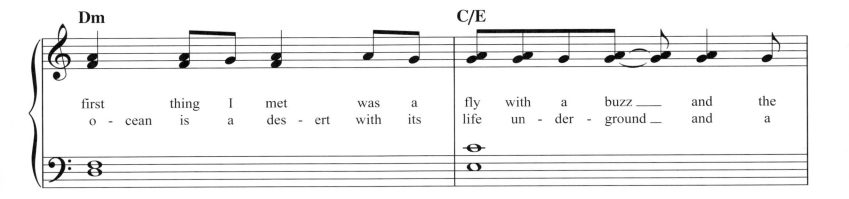

first thing I met was a fly with a buzz ____ and the
o - cean is a des - ert with its life un - der - ground ____ and a

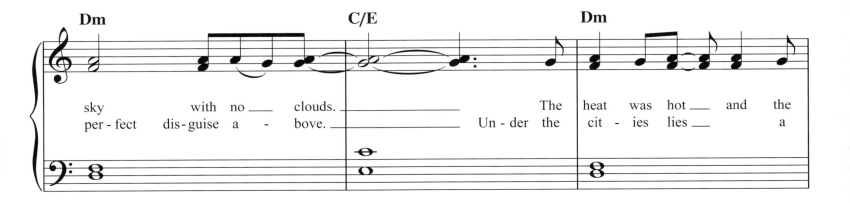

sky with no ____ clouds. ____ The heat was hot ____ and the
per - fect dis - guise a - bove. ____ Un - der the cit - ies lies ____ a

ground was dry, ____ but the air was full ____ of ____ sound.
heart made of ground ____ but the hu - mans will give ____ no ____ love.

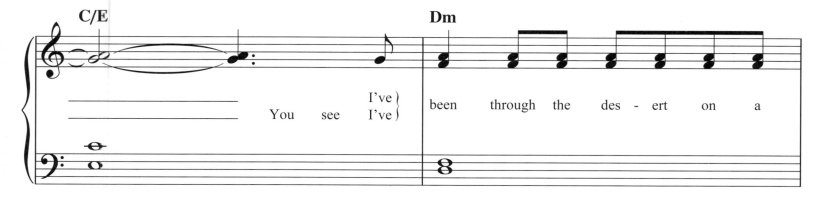

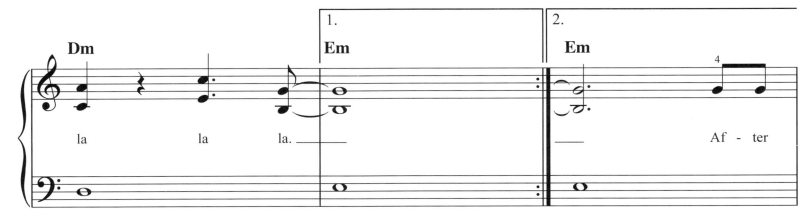

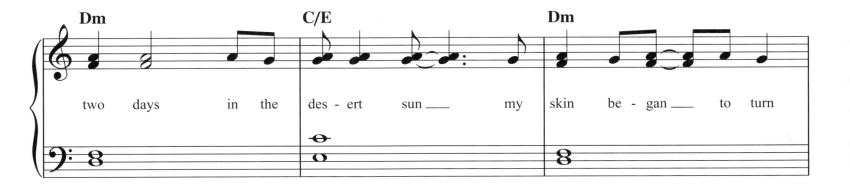

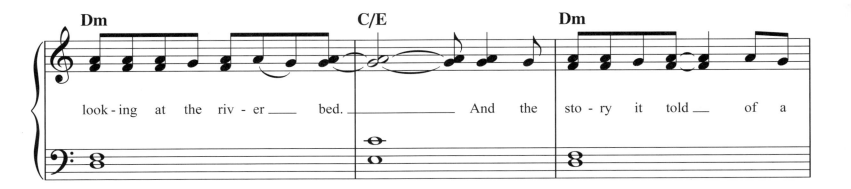

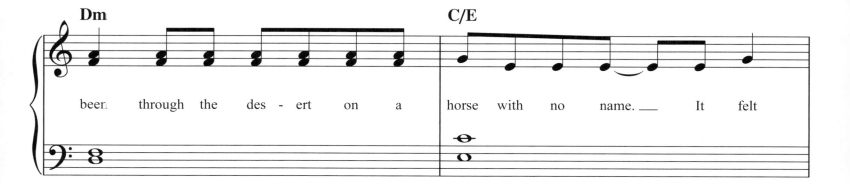

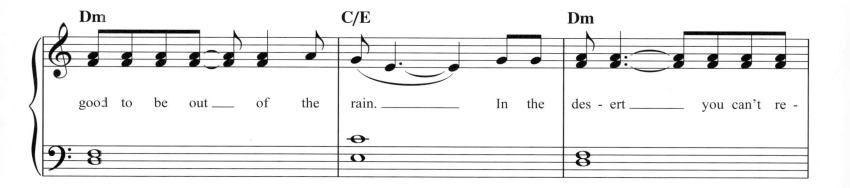

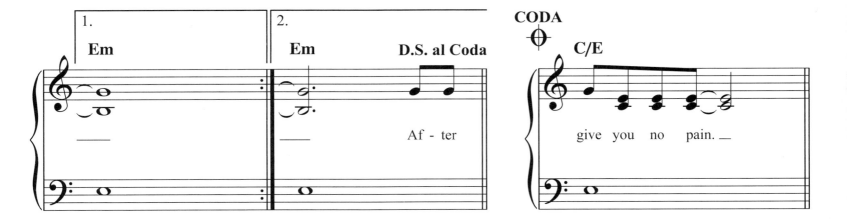

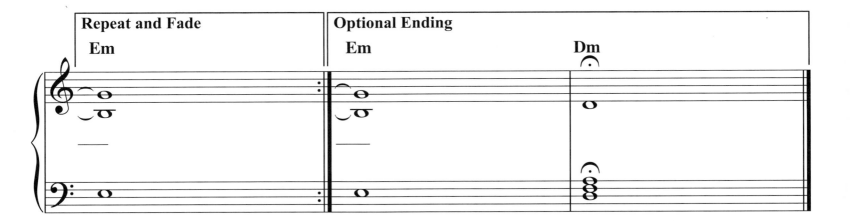

HOTEL CALIFORNIA

Words and Music by DON HENLEY,
GLENN FREY and DON FELDER

Moderate Rock

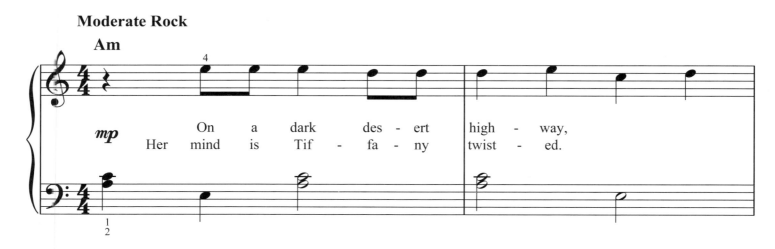

On a dark des - ert high - way,
Her mind is Tif - fa - ny twist - ed.

cool wind in my hair,
She got the Mer - ce - des bends.

warm smell of co -
She got a lot of pret - ty,

li - tas rising up through the air.
pret - ty boys she calls friends.

F   C

Up a - head in the dis - tance,
How they dance in the court - yard;

I saw a shim - mer - ing
sweet __ sum - mer

Dm

light.
sweat.

My head grew heav - y and my sight grew dim; __
Some __ dance __ to re - mem - ber; __

E7   Am

I had to stop for the night. _____
some __ dance to for - get. _____

There she stood in the
So I called up the

E7

door - way;
cap - tain:

I heard the mis - sion bell. ___
"Please bring me my wine."

He said,

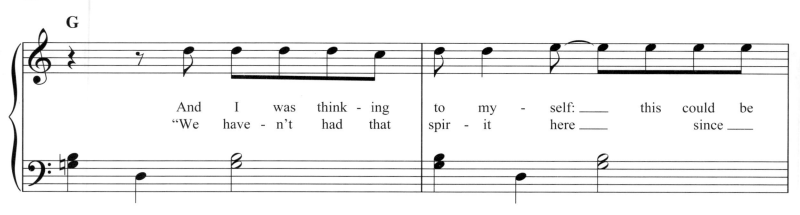

And I was think - ing to my - self: ____ this could be
"We have - n't had that spir - it here ____ since ____

heav - en or this could be hell. _____ Then she lit up a
nine - teen six - ty - nine." ____ And still ____ those

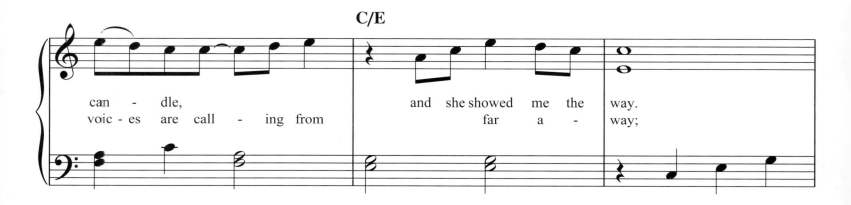

can - dle, and she showed me the way.
voic - es are call - ing from far a - way;

There were voic - es down the cor - ri - dor; ____ I thought I heard them
wake you up ____ in the mid-dle of the night just to hear them

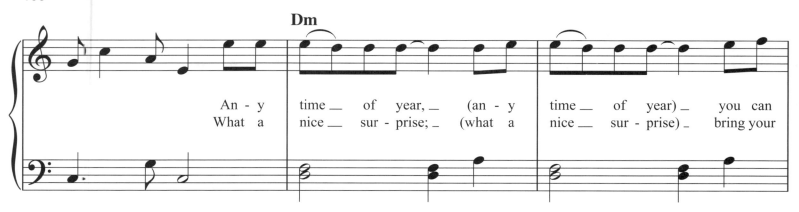

Any time of year, (an-y time of year) you can
What a nice surprise; (what a nice surprise) bring your

1.
find it here."

2.
al - i - bis."

Mir - rors on the ceil - ing,
Last thing I re - mem - ber I was

the pink cham - pagne on ice, and she said,
run - ning for the door.

"We are all just
I had to find the

pris - on - ers here ___ of our own ___ de - vice."
pas - sage back to the place I was ___ be - fore.

And in the mas - ter's ___ cham - bers, ___ they gath - ered for the
"Re - lax," said the night man. ___ "We are pro - grammed to re -

feast. They stab it ___ with their steel - y knives, _ but they
ceive. You can check out an - y time you like, ___ but

just can't ___ kill the beast.
you can ___ nev - er leave."

I WALK THE LINE

Words and Music by
JOHN R. CASH

Bright Country 2-beat

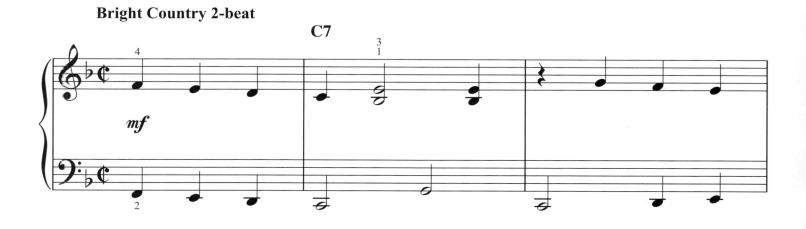

I keep a close watch
night is
close watch

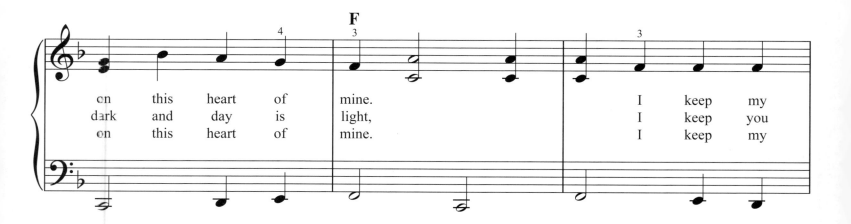

on this heart of mine. I keep my
dark and day is light, I keep you
on this day heart of mine. I keep my

C7 ... **F**

eyes   wide   o - pen   all   the   time.
on   my   mind   both   day   and   night.
eyes   wide   o - pen   all   the   time.

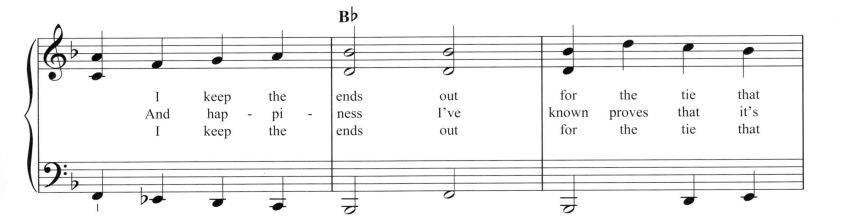

Bb

I   keep   the   ends   out   for   the   tie   that
And   hap - pi - ness   I've   known   proves   that   it's
I   keep   the   ends   out   for   the   tie   that

F ... **C7**

binds.
right.   Be - cause   you're   mine
binds.   Be - cause   you're   mine
       Be - cause   you're   mine

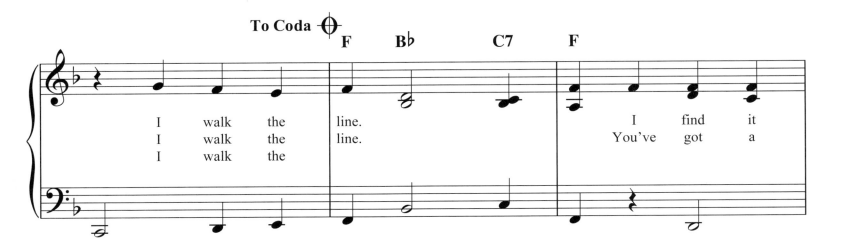

To Coda ⊕   **F**   **Bb**   **C7**   **F**

I   walk   the   line.
I   walk   the   line.   I   find   it
I   walk   the   You've   got   a

ver - y   eas - y   to   be   true.
way   to   keep   me   on   your   side.

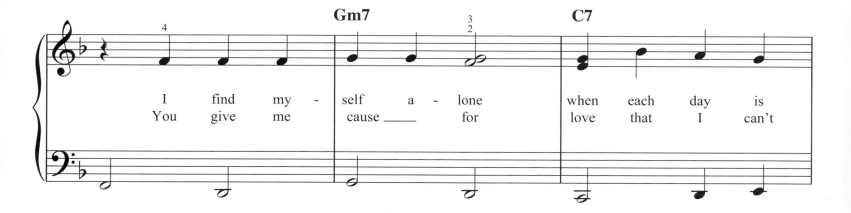

I   find   my - self   a - lone   when   each   day   is
You   give   me   cause _____ for   love   that   I   can't

through.   Yes,   I'll   ad - mit   that
hide.   For   you   I   know   I'd

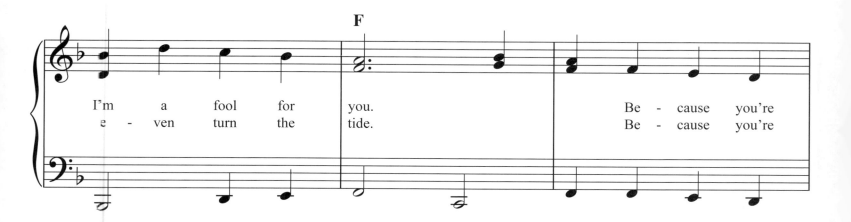

I'm   a   fool   for   you.   Be - cause   you're
e - ven   turn   for   the   tide.   Be - cause   you're

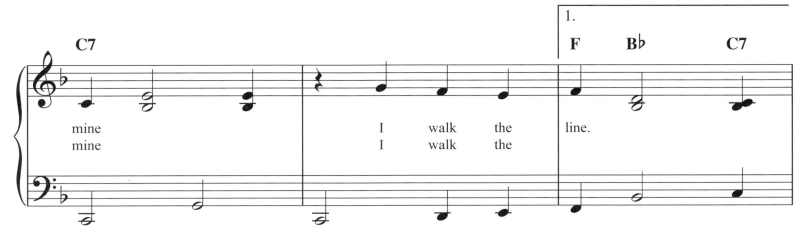

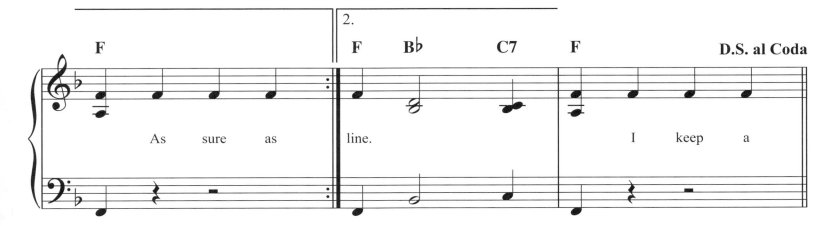

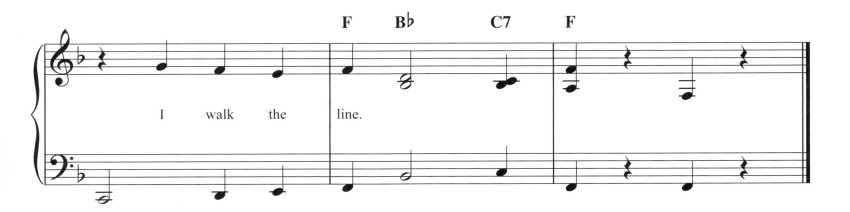

I'M YOURS

Words and Music by
JASON MRAZ

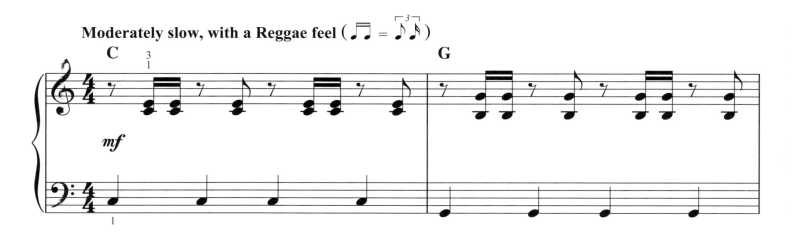

1. Well,
2. *(See additional lyrics)*

you done done me in; you bet I felt it. I tried to be chill, but you're so hot that I melt-ed. I

fell right through the cracks. _ Now I'm try-ing to get back. ___ Be-fore the

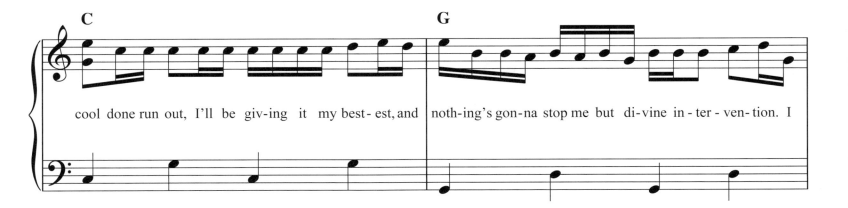

cool done run out, I'll be giv-ing it my best-est, and noth-ing's gon-na stop me but di-vine in-ter-ven-tion. I

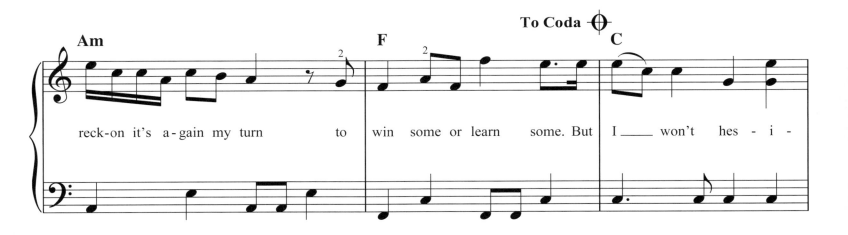

reck-on it's a-gain my turn to win some or learn some. But I ___ won't hes-i-

tate no more, no ___ more. _ It can-not wait. I'm yours. ___

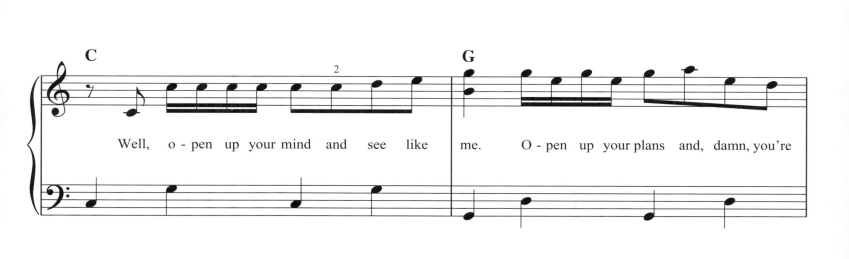

Well, o - pen up your mind and see like me. O - pen up your plans and, damn, you're

free. Look in - to your heart ___ and you'll find love, love, _____ love.

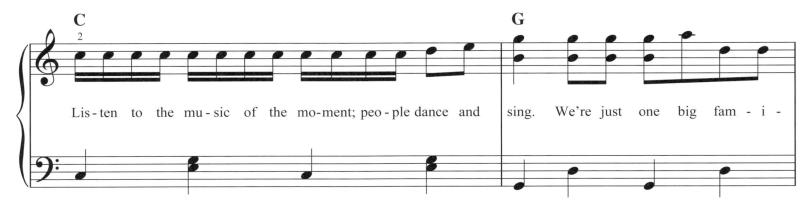

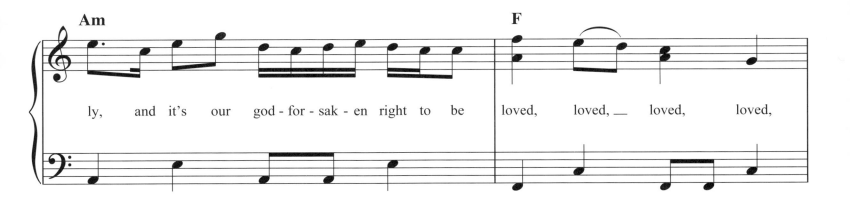

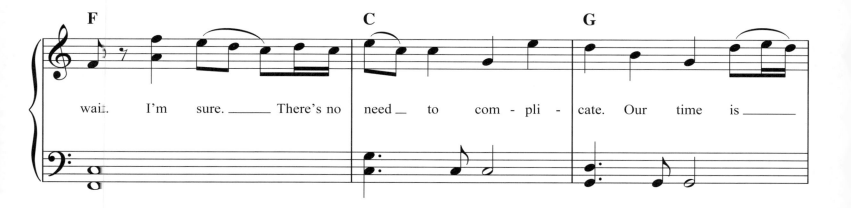

Additional Lyrics

2. I've been spending way too long
Checking my tongue in the mirror
And bending over backwards
Just to try to see it clearer.
But my breath fogged up the glass,
And so I drew a new face and I laughed.
I guess what I'll be saying
Is there ain't no better reason
To rid yourself of vanities
And just go with the seasons.
It's what we aim to do.
Our name is our virtue.

But I won't hesitate no more...

THE IMPOSSIBLE DREAM

(The Quest)
from MAN OF LA MANCHA

Lyric by JOE DARION
Music by MITCH LEIGH

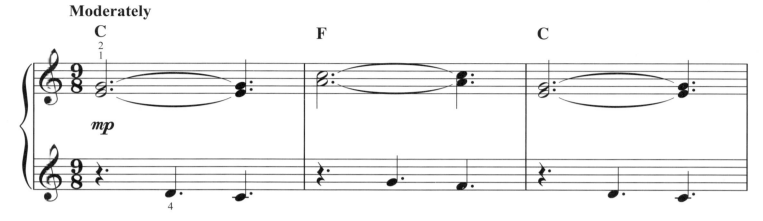

To dream ___ the im-pos-si-ble dream, ___ to

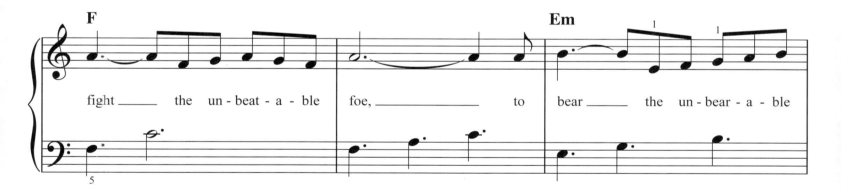

fight ___ the un-beat-a-ble foe, ___ to bear ___ the un-bear-a-ble

sor-row, ___ to run ___ where the brave dare not go. ___ To

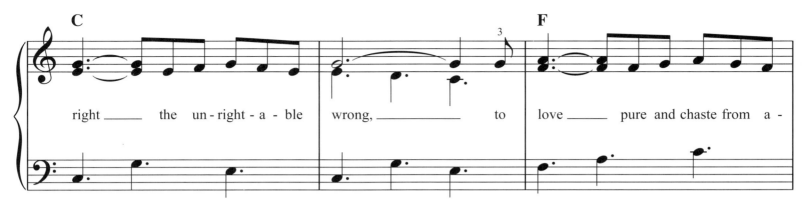

right _____ the un-right-a-ble wrong, _____ to love _____ pure and chaste from a-

far, _____ to try _____ when your arms are too wear-y, _____ to

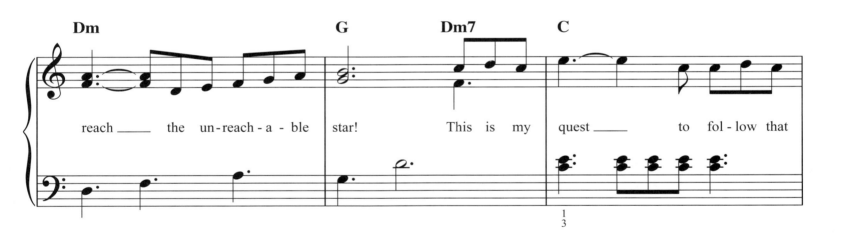

reach _____ the un-reach-a-ble star! This is my quest _____ to fol-low that

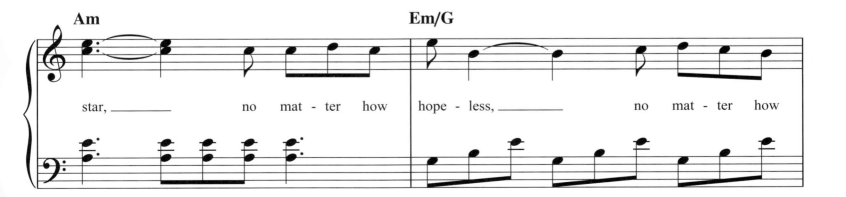

star, _____ no mat-ter how hope-less, _____ no mat-ter how

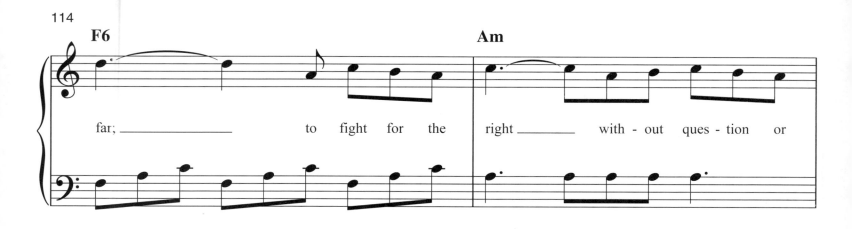

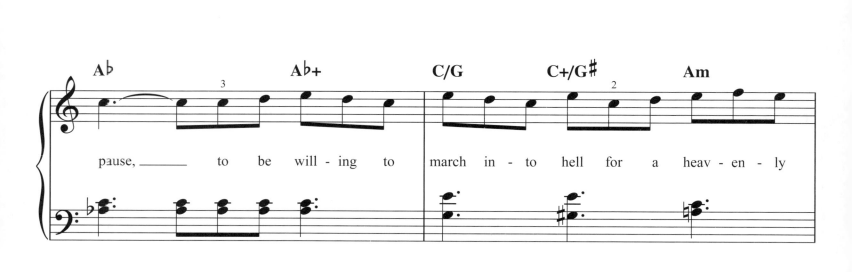

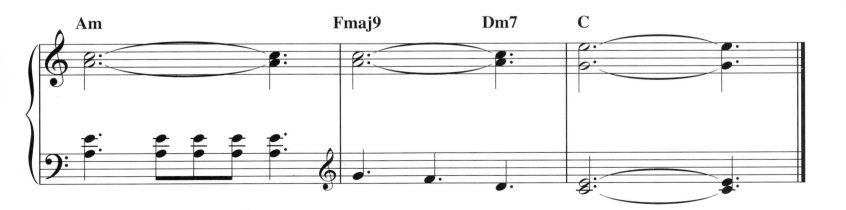

JUST THE WAY YOU ARE

Words and Music by BRUNO MARS,
ARI LEVINE, PHILIP LAWRENCE,
KHARI CAIN and KHALIL WALTON

Moderate Hip-Hop groove

Oh, her eyes, _ her eyes _ make the

stars look like they're not shin-in'. Her hair, _ her hair _ falls per-fect-ly with-out her try-in'.

She's so beau-ti-ful, and I tell her ev-'ry day.

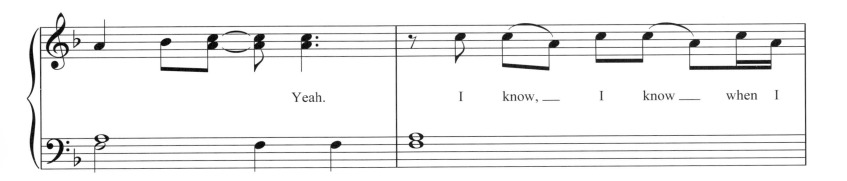

Yeah. I know, ___ I know ___ when I

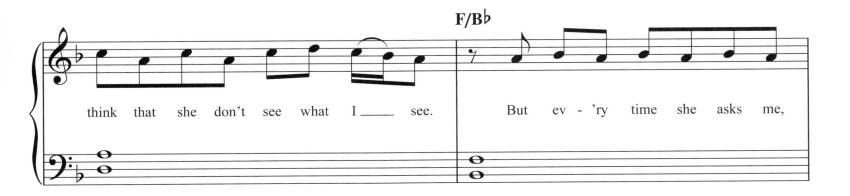

com-pli-ment her, she won't be-lieve ___ me. And it's so, ___ it's so ___ sad to

think that she don't see what I ___ see. But ev-'ry time she asks me,

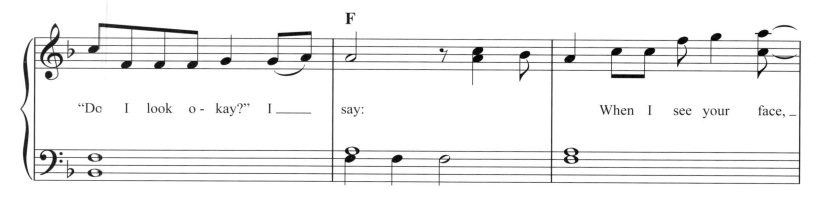

"Do I look o-kay?" I ____ say: When I see your face, ____

____ there's not a thing ____ that I ____ would change, ____

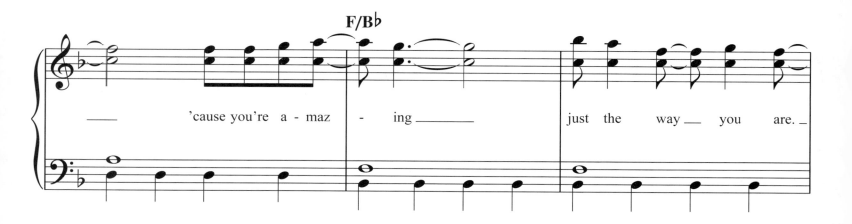

____ 'cause you're a-maz ____ -ing ____ just the way ____ you are. ____

____ And when you smile, ____

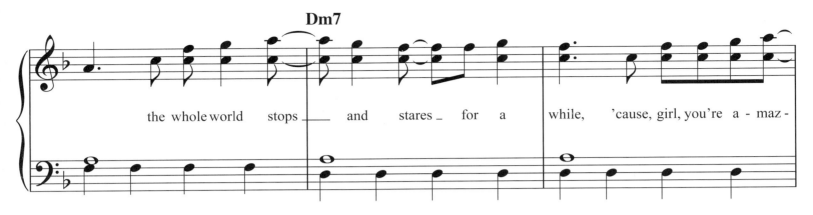

Dm7

the whole world stops __ and stares __ for a while, 'cause, girl, you're a - maz-

F/B♭   **F**   **To Coda** ⊕

- ing _____ just the way __ you are. __

Yeah. __ Her lips, __ her lips, __ I could kiss them all day if she'd let me.

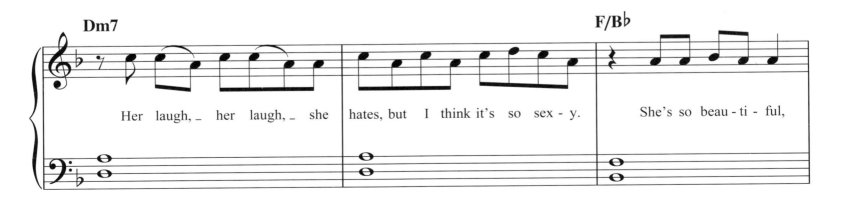

Dm7   **F/B♭**

Her laugh, __ her laugh, __ she hates, but I think it's so sex - y. She's so beau - ti - ful,

and I tell her ev - 'ry day.   Oh,   you

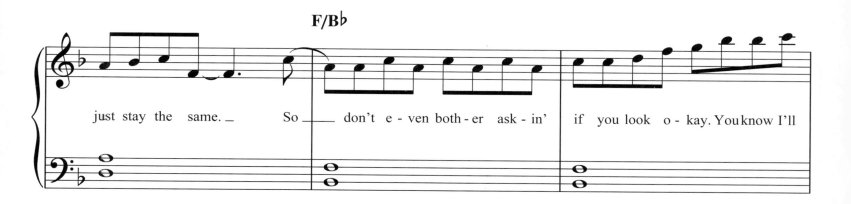

know, you know, you know I'd nev - er | ask you to   change. _   If | per-fect's what you're search-in' for, then

just stay the   same. _   So __ don't e - ven both - er   ask - in' | if you look o - kay. You know I'll

say: _____ | When I   see your   face, _

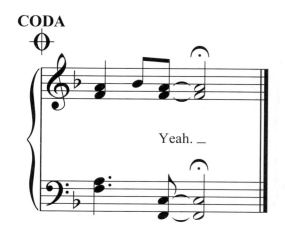

Yeah. _

LEAN ON ME

Words and Music by
BILL WITHERS

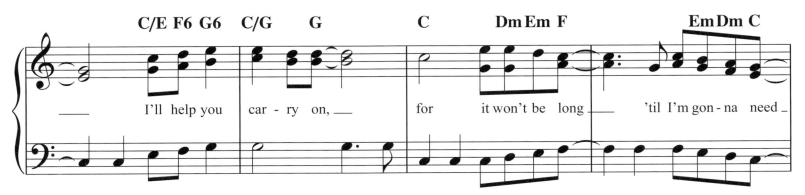

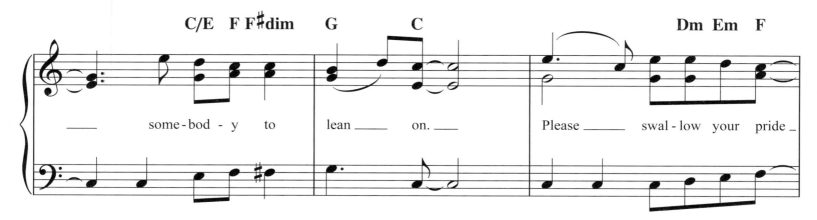

LET IT BE

Words and Music by JOHN LENNON
and PAUL McCARTNEY

Slowly, in 2

When I find my-self in times of trou-ble, Moth-er Mar-y
Instrumental

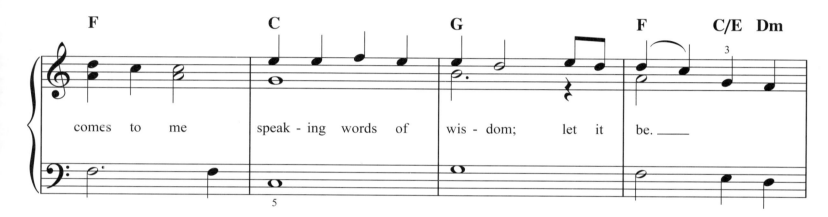

comes to me speak-ing words of wis-dom; let it be. ___

And in my hour of dark-ness she is stand-ing right in

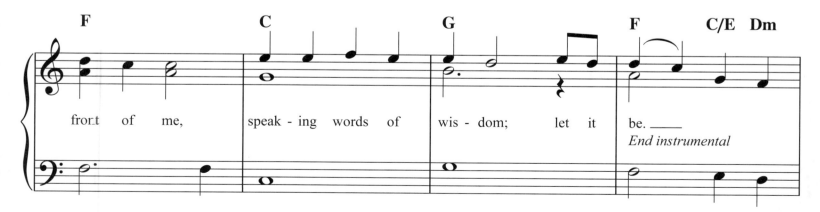

front of me, speak-ing words of wis-dom; let it be. ___
End instrumental

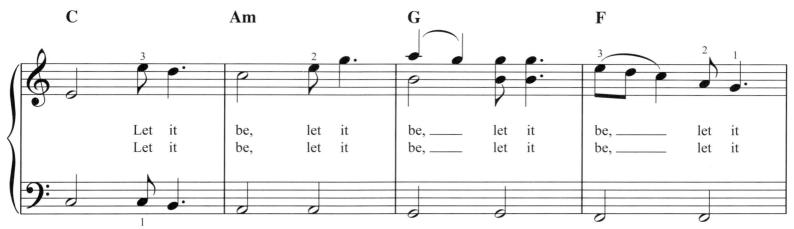

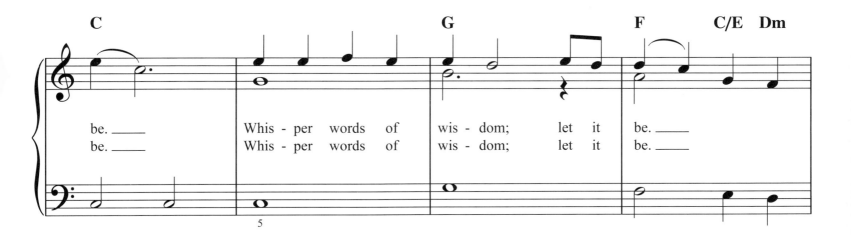

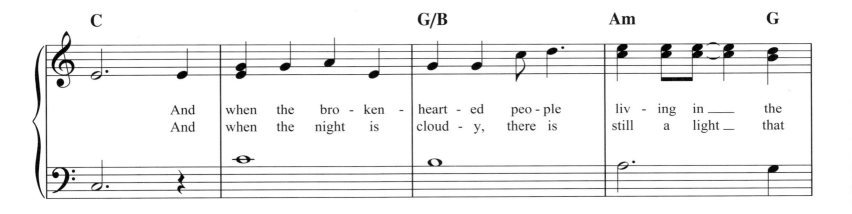

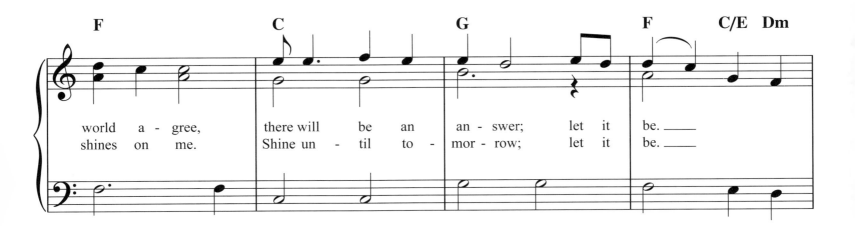

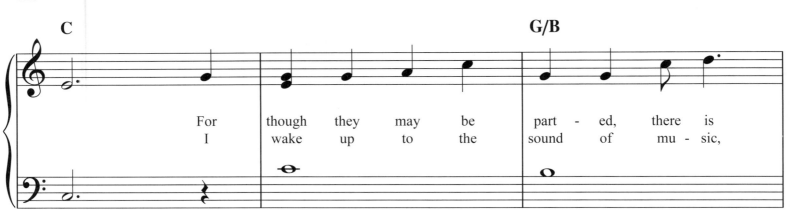

For though they may be part - ed, there is
I wake up to the sound of mu - sic,

still a chance that they will see, there will be an
Moth - er Mar - y comes to me, speak - ing words of

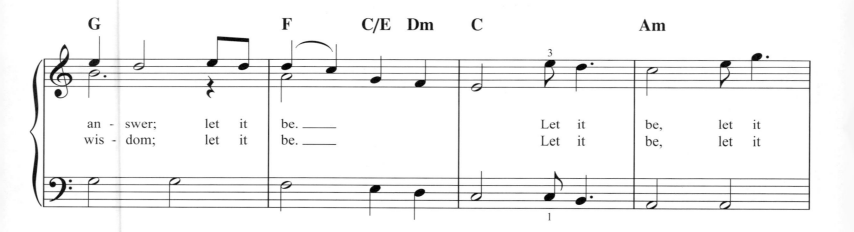

an - swer; let it be. ___ Let it be, let it
wis - dom; let it be. ___ Let it be, let it

be, ___ let it be, ___ let it be. ___ There will be an
be, ___ let it be, ___ let it be. ___ There will be an

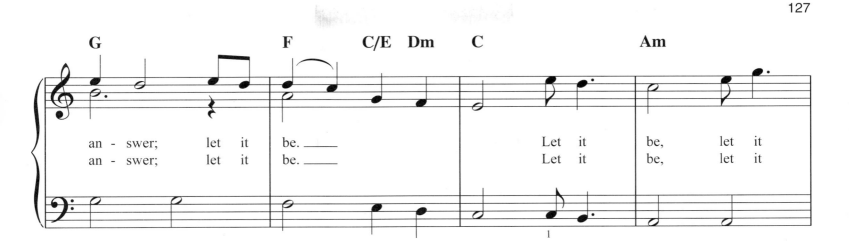

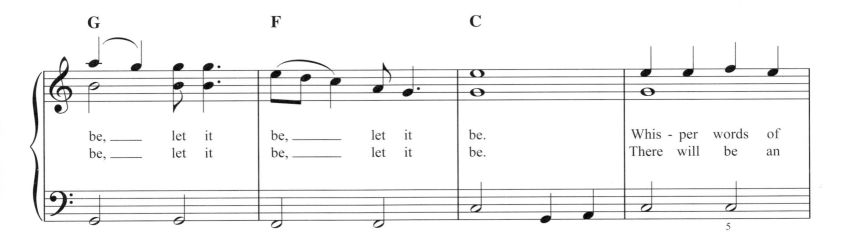

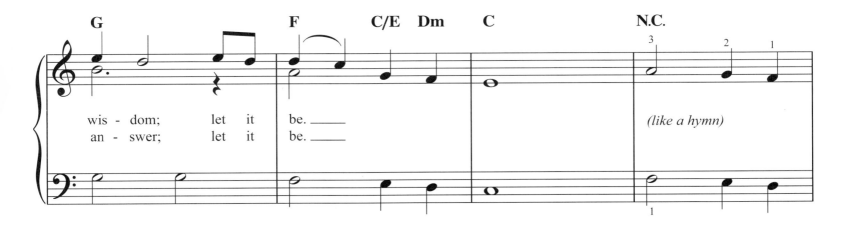

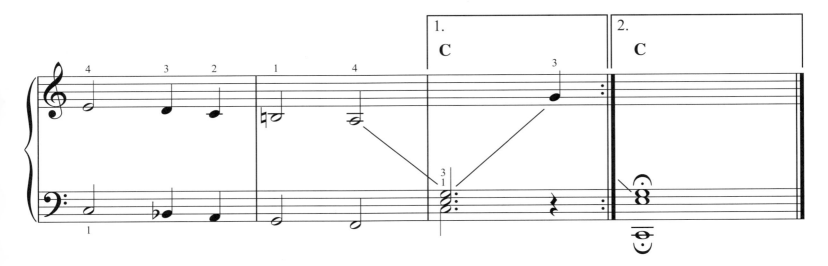

LET IT GO
from FROZEN

Music and Lyrics by KRISTEN ANDERSON-LOPEZ
and ROBERT LOPEZ

Half-time feel, mysterious

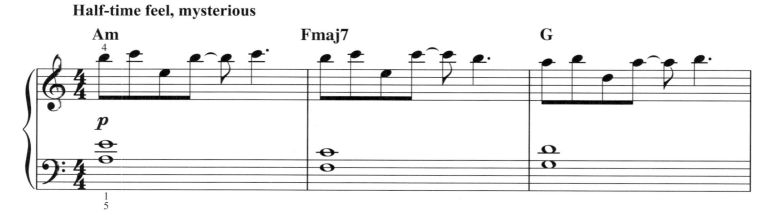

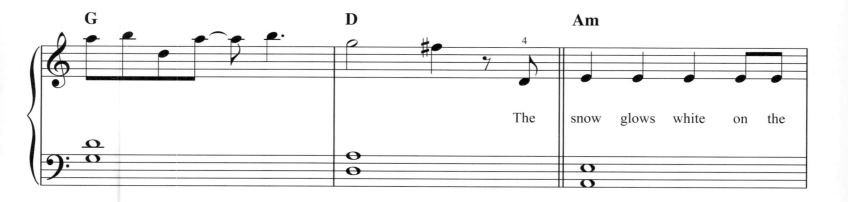

The snow glows white on the

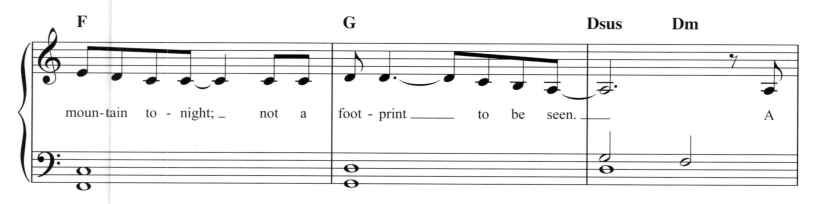

moun-tain to-night;___ not a foot-print _____ to be seen.___ A

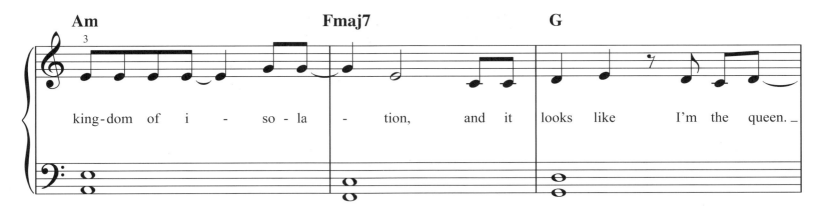

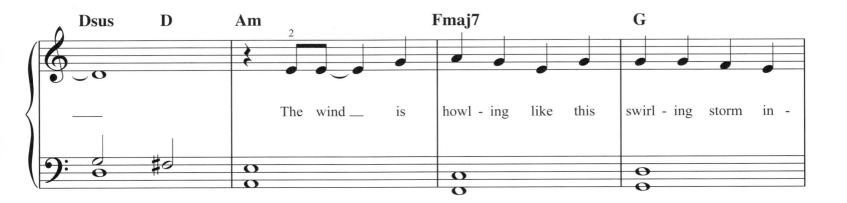

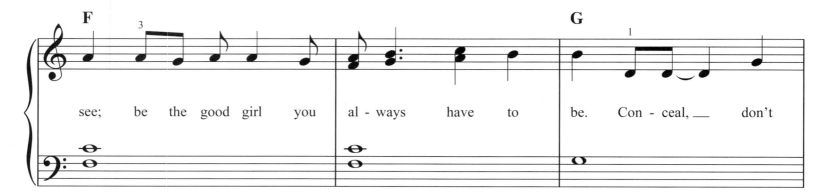

let it go; ___ turn a - way ___ and slam ___ the ___
let it go; ___ you'll nev \- er see ___ me ___

door. ___ I don't ___ care ___ what they're
cry. ___ Here I ___ stand, ___ and

going to ___ say; ___ let the storm rage ___ on. ___
here I'll ___ stay; ___ let the storm rage ___ on. ___

___ The cold nev - er both - ered me an - y - way.

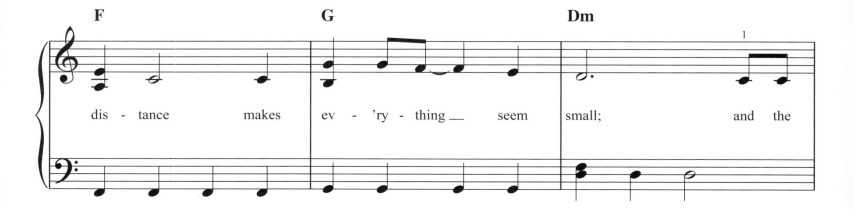

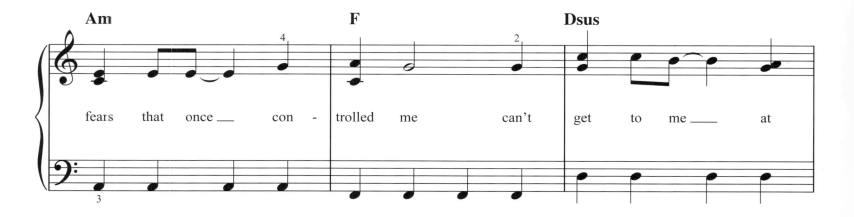

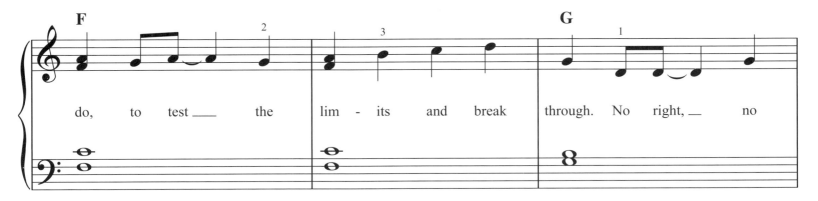

do, to test ___ the lim - its and break through. No right, ___ no

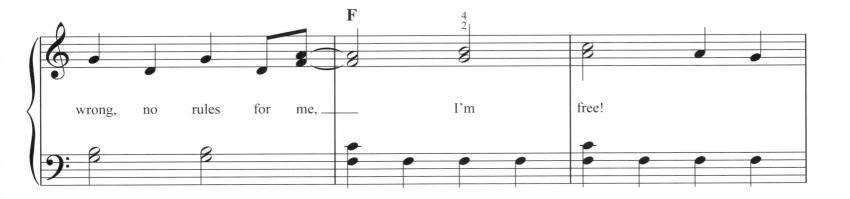

wrong, no rules for me, ___ I'm free!

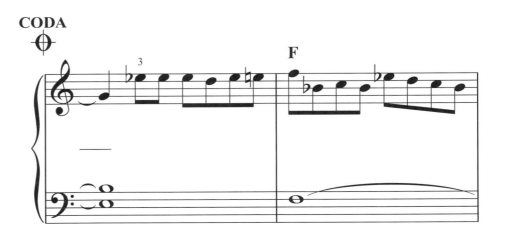

Let it go, ___

My pow — er   flur - ries through the   air   in - to the

grou_nd.   My soul __ is   spi - ral - ing   in

fro - zen   frac - tals   all a - round. _   **G**   And one __ thought

cry - stal - liz - es   like   an   i - cy   blast:

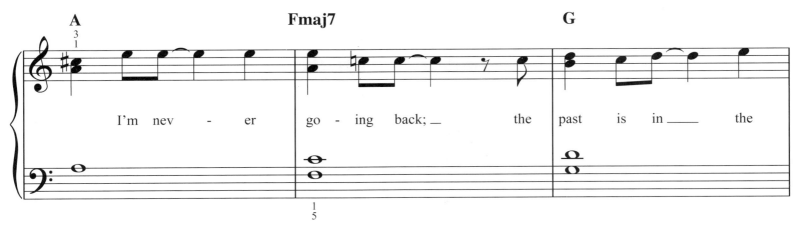

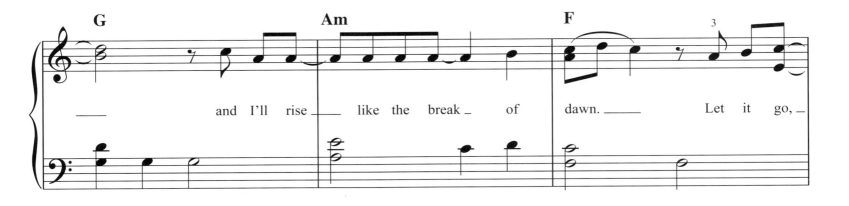

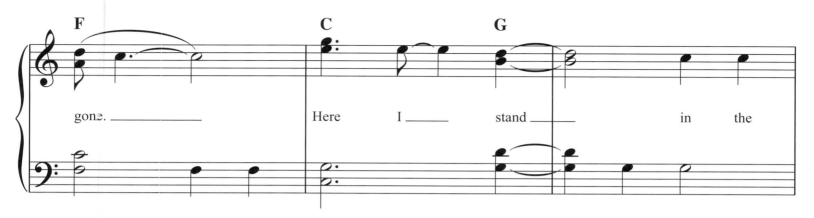

gone. _____ Here I _____ stand _____ in the

light of _____ day; _____ let the

storm rage _____ on. _____ The

cold nev - er both - ered me an - y - way. _____

LOVE STORY

Words and Music by
TAYLOR SWIFT

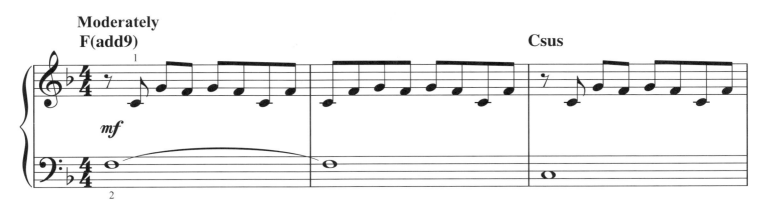

Lyrics:
We were both young when I first saw ___ you. I close my eyes ___ and the flash-back starts. ___ I'm stand-in'

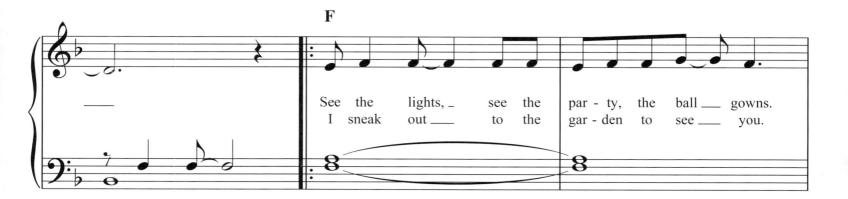

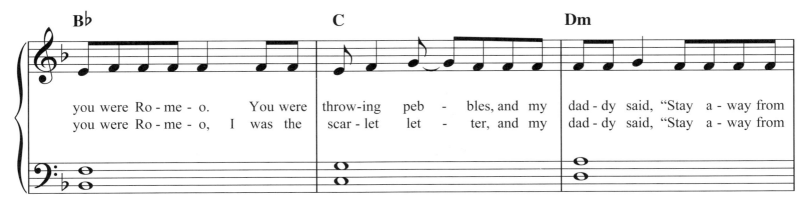

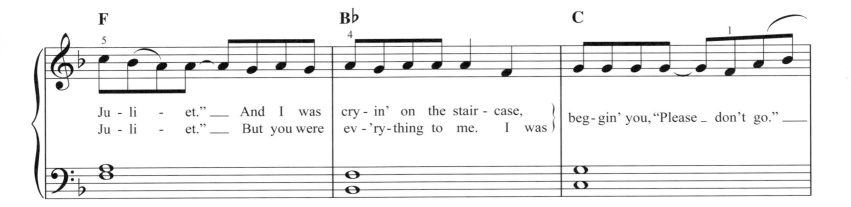

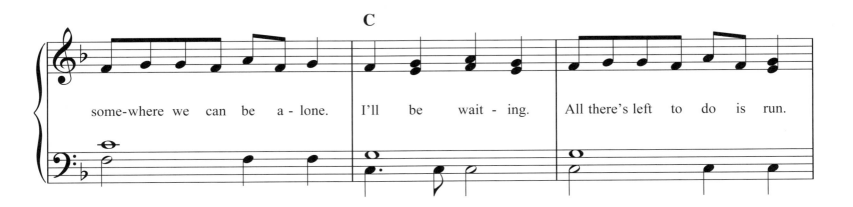

You'll be the prince and I'll be the prin - cess. It's a love sto - ry. ___

Ba - by, just say ___ yes." So

"Ro - me - o, save me. They're try'n' to tell me how to feel. This love is dif - fi - cult,

but it's ___ real. ___ Don't be a - fraid. We'll make it out of this mess.

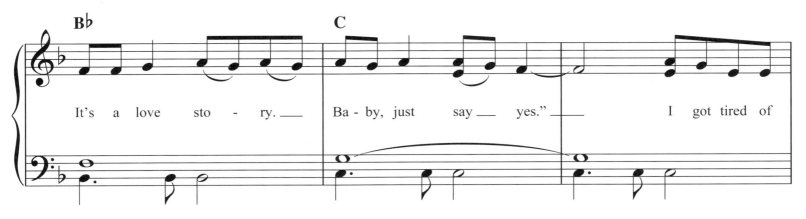

It's a love sto - ry. ___ Ba - by, just say ___ yes." ___ I got tired of

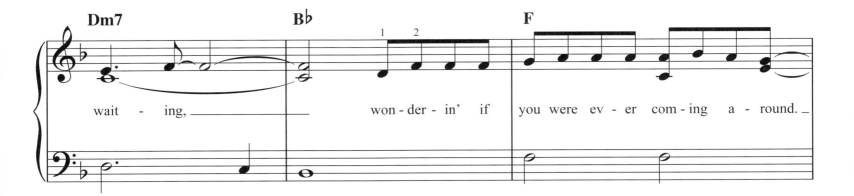

wait - ing, ___ ___ won - der - in' if you were ev - er com - ing a - round. ___

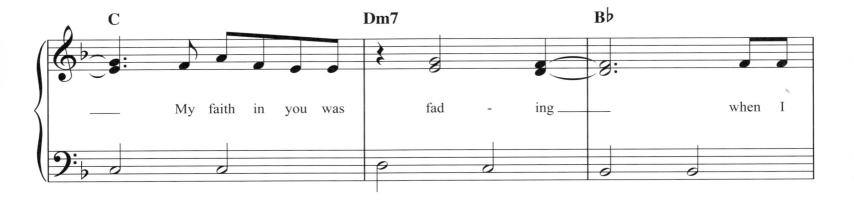

___ My faith in you was fad - ing ___ when I

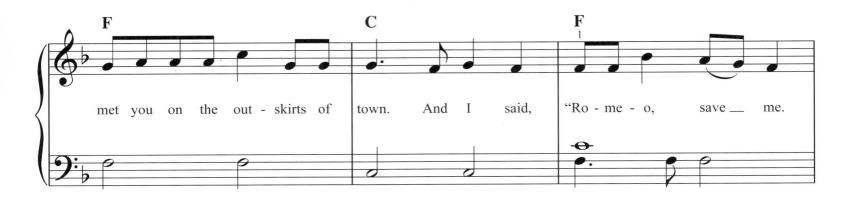

met you on the out - skirts of town. And I said, "Ro - me - o, save ___ me.

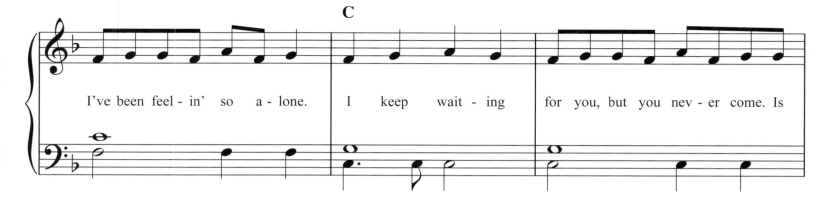

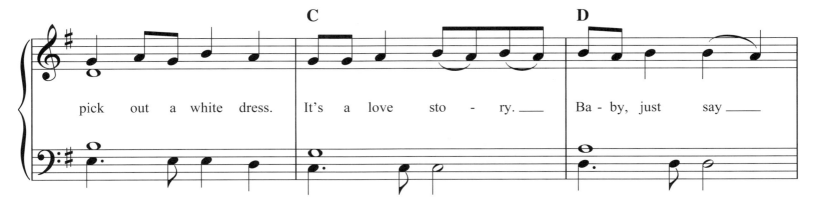

pick out a white dress. It's a love sto - ry. ___ Ba - by, just say ___

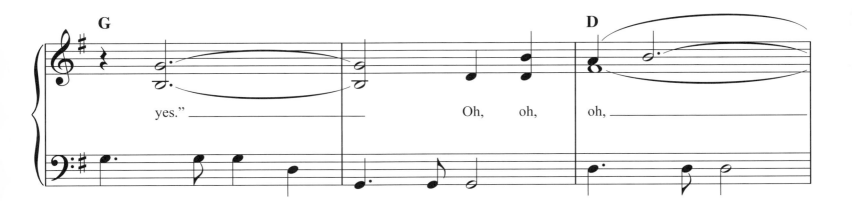

yes." ___ Oh, oh, oh, ___

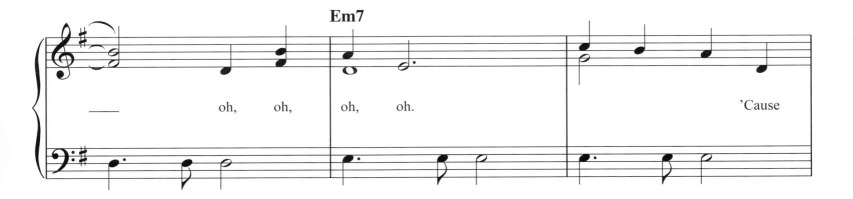

___ oh, oh, oh, oh. 'Cause

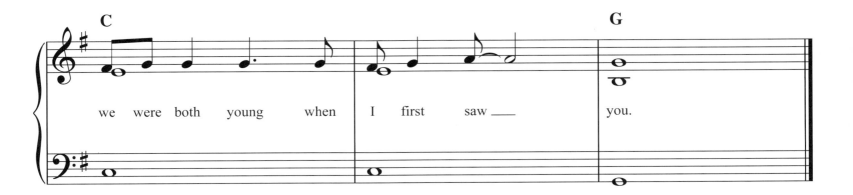

we were both young when I first saw ___ you.

THE LUCKIEST

Words and Music by
BEN FOLDS

Freely with sentiment

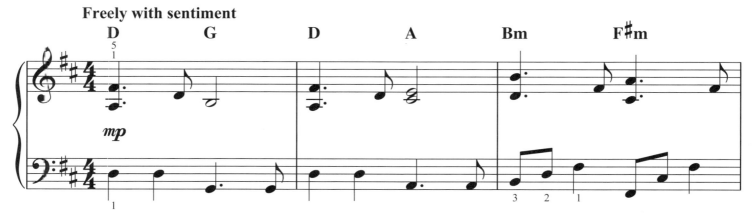

1. I don't get man-y things right the first time. In
2.-3. *(See additional lyrics)*

fact, I am told that a lot. Now I know all ___ the wrong turns, ___ the

stum - bles ___ and falls brought ___ me here.

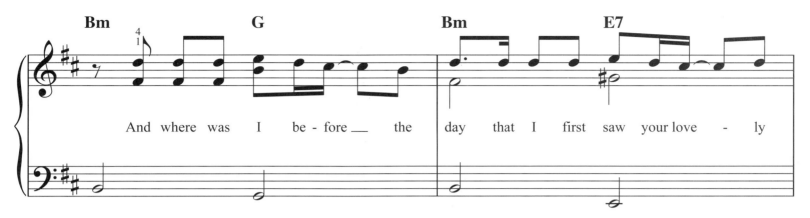

And where was I be - fore ___ the day that I first saw your love - ly

face? Now I see it ev-'ry day and I ___ know that

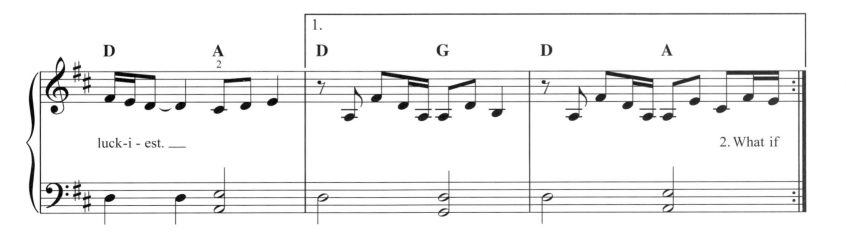

I am, I am, I am the

luck-i - est. ___

2. What if

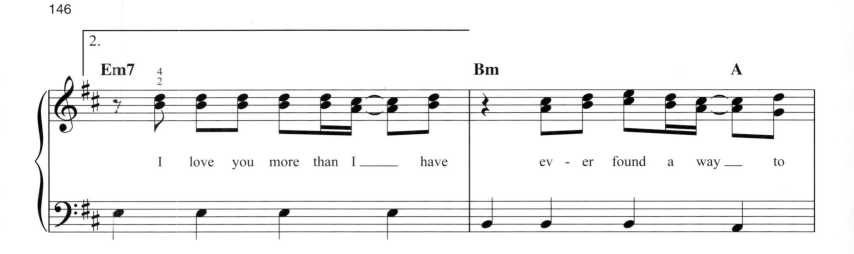

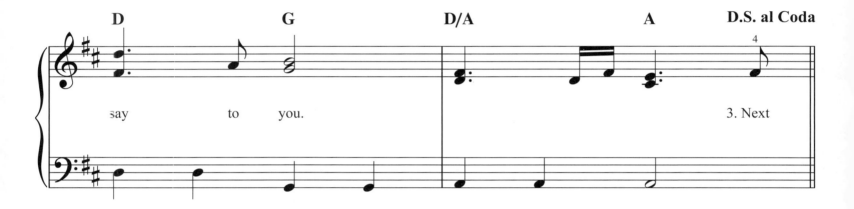

Additional Lyrics

2. What if I'd been born fifty years before you
   In a house on the street where you live?
   Maybe I'd be outside as you passed on your bike,
   Would I know?
   In a wide sea of eyes I see one pair that I recognize
   And I know that I am, I am, I am the luckiest.

3. Next door there's an old man who lived into his nineties
   And one day passed away in his sleep.
   And his wife, she stayed for a couple of days
   And passed away. I'm sorry I know
   That's a strange way to tell you that I know we belong,
   That I know that I am, I am, I am the luckiest.

MAN IN THE MIRROR

Words and Music by GLEN BALLARD
and SIEDAH GARRETT

Moderately

I'm gon-na make a change _ for once in my life.

It's gon-na feel real _ good, _ gon-na make a dif-f'rence, gon-na make it right. _

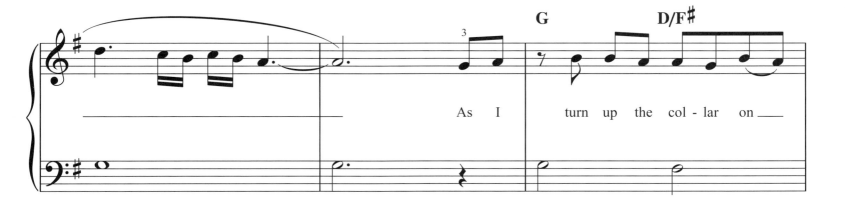

_____ As I turn up the col-lar on _____

my fa-v'rite win-ter coat, _ this wind is blow-in' my mind. _ I see the kids _

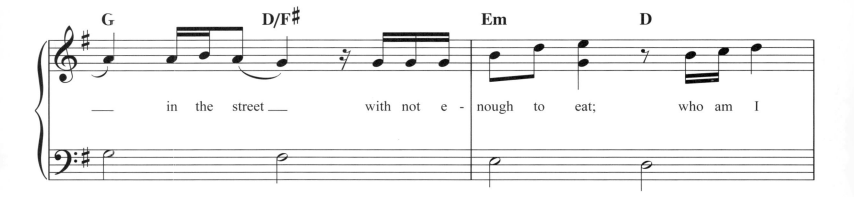

_ in the street _ with not e - nough to eat; who am I

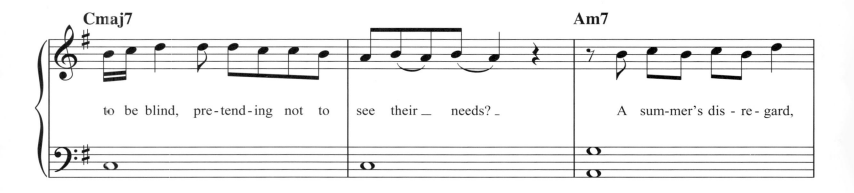

to be blind, pre-tend-ing not to see their _ needs? _ A sum-mer's dis - re - gard,

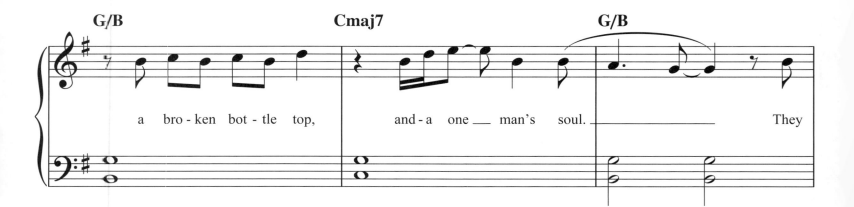

a bro-ken bot-tle top, and-a one _ man's soul. _ They

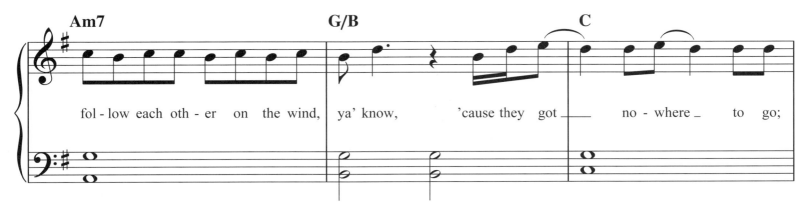

fol - low each oth - er on the wind, ya' know, 'cause they got ___ no - where _ to go;

that's why I want you to know. I'm start - ing with the man __ in the mir - ror,

I'm ask - ing him to change _ his ways. _ And no ___ mes - sage could have

been an - y clear - er: If you wan - na make the world a bet - ter place, _ take a

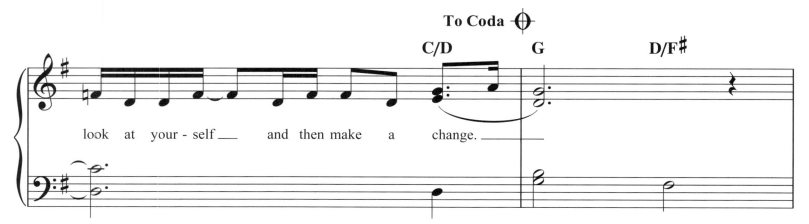

look at your-self ___ and then make a change. ___

Na na na na na na na na ___ na nah. ___

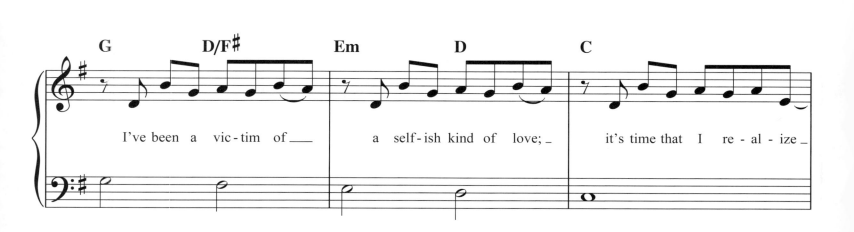

I've been a vic-tim of ___ a self-ish kind of love; ___ it's time that I re-al-ize ___

___ that there are some with no home, ___ not a nick-el to loan; could it be

real-ly me pre-tend-ing that they're not a - lone? _ A wil-low deep-ly scarred,

some-bod-y's bro-ken heart and a washed - out dream. _____ They

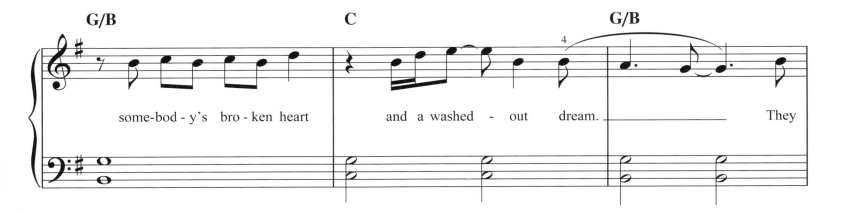

fol-low the pat-tern of the wind, ya see, 'cause they got ___ no place _ to be;

that's why I'm start-ing with me.

MOON RIVER

from the Paramount Picture BREAKFAST AT TIFFANY'S

Words by JOHNNY MERCER
Music by HENRY MANCINI

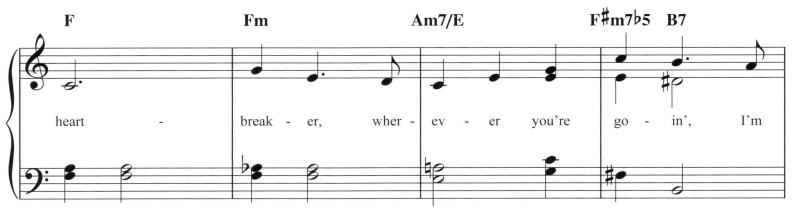

heart - break - er, wher - ev - er you're go - in', I'm

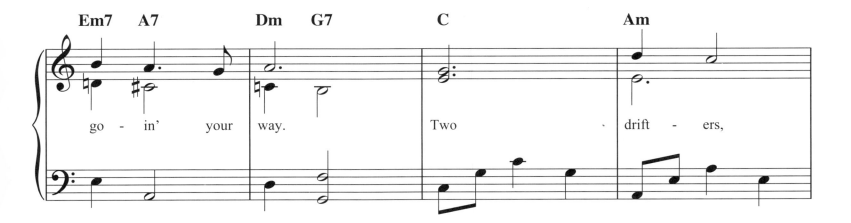

go - in' your way. Two drift - ers,

off to see the world. There's such a lot of world to

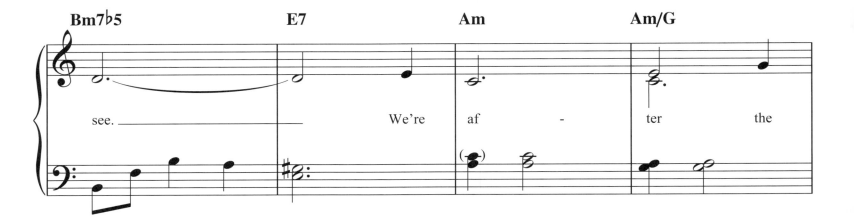

see. ____ We're af - ter the

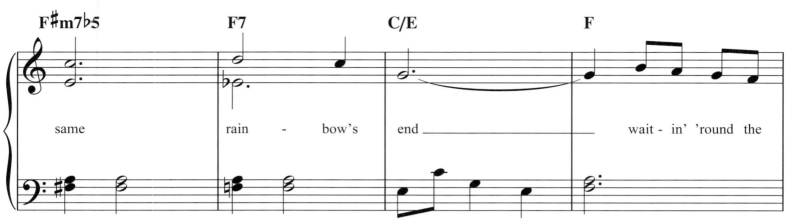

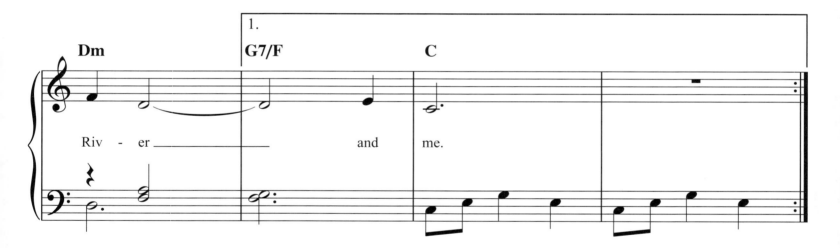

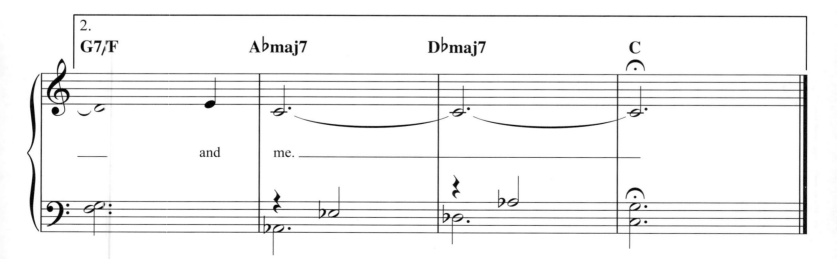

OVER THE RAINBOW

from THE WIZARD OF OZ

Music by HAROLD ARLEN
Lyric by E.Y. "YIP" HARBURG

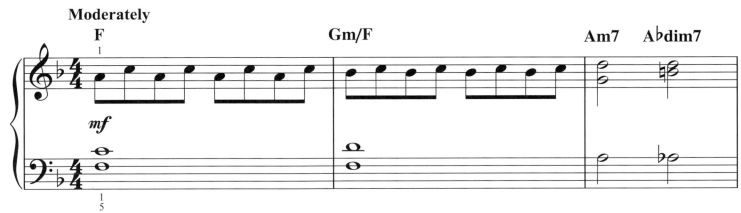

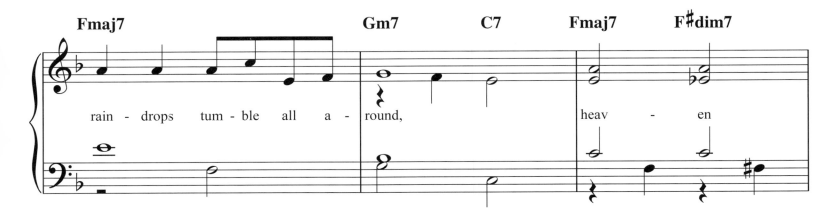

When all the world is a hope-less jum-ble and the

rain-drops tum-ble all a - round, heav - en

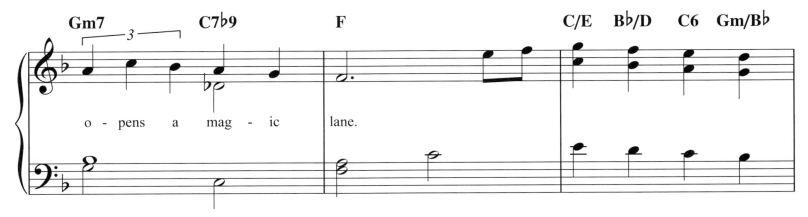

o - pens a mag - ic lane.

When all the clouds dark-en up the sky-way, there's a rain-bow high-way to be

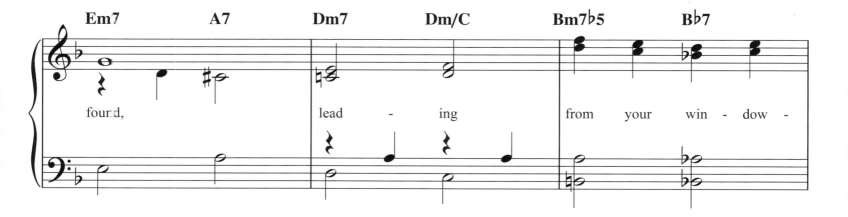

found, lead - ing from your win-dow -

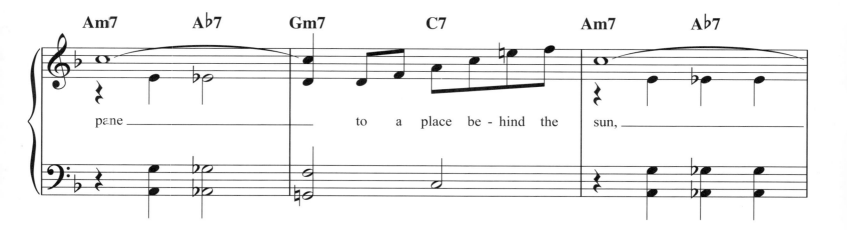

pane _____ to a place be-hind the sun, _____

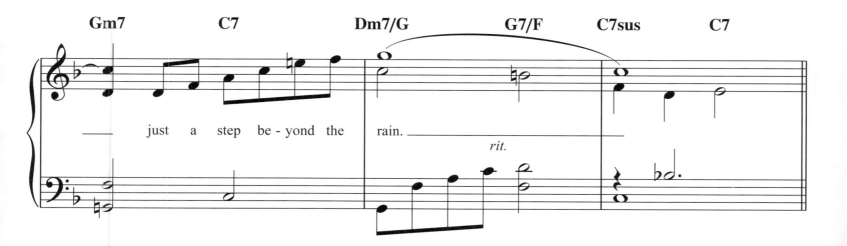

_____ just a step be-yond the rain. _____

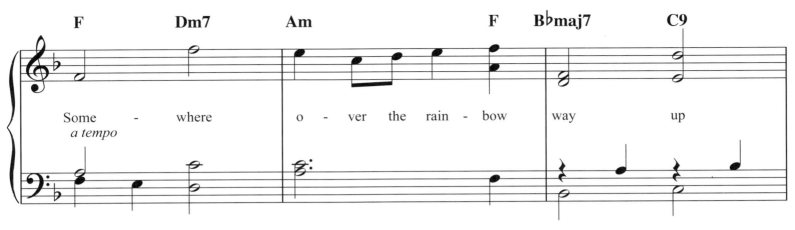

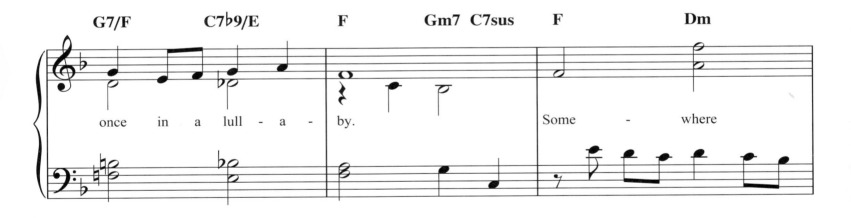

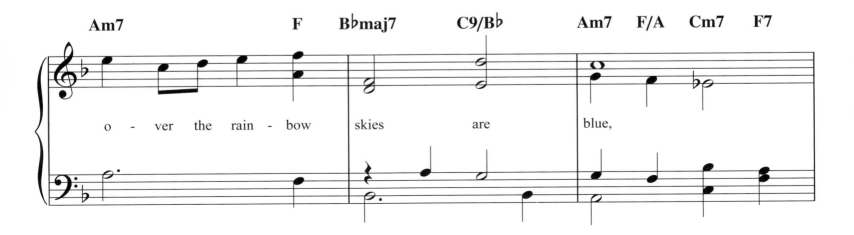

and the dreams that you dare to dream real - ly do come

true. _____ Some - day I'll wish up - on a star and wake up where the clouds are far be -

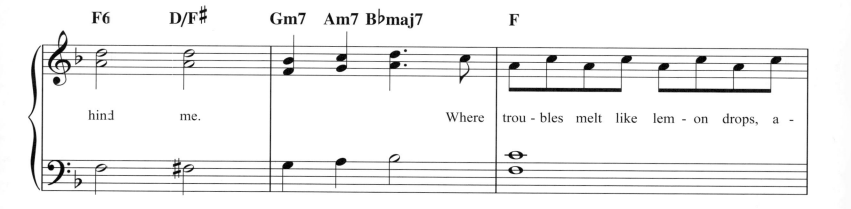

hind me. Where trou - bles melt like lem - on drops, a -

way, a - bove the chim - ney tops that's where you'll find me.

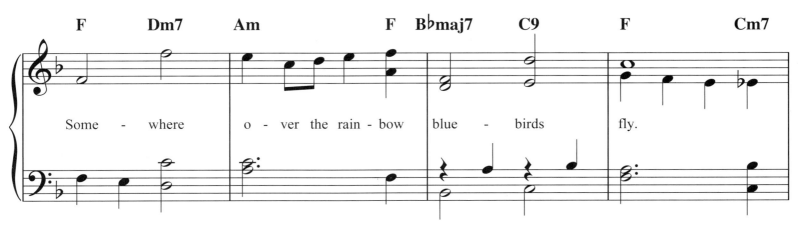

Some - where o - ver the rain - bow blue - birds fly.

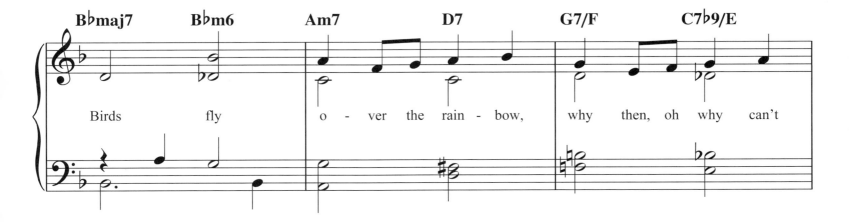

Birds fly o - ver the rain - bow, why then, oh why can't

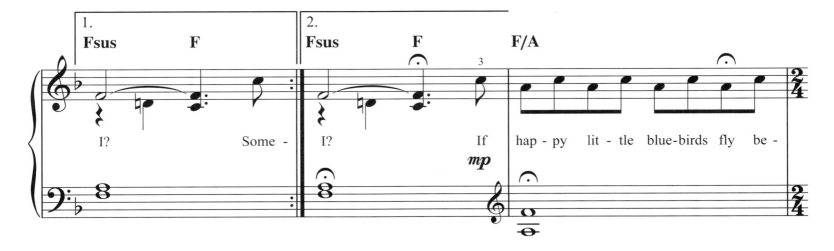

I? Some - I? If hap - py lit - tle blue-birds fly be -

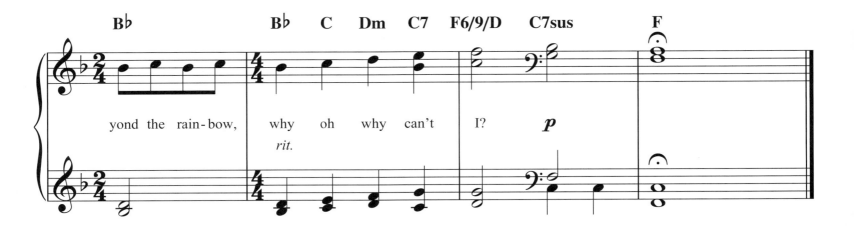

yond the rain-bow, why oh why can't I?

TAKE ME HOME, COUNTRY ROADS

Words and Music by JOHN DENVER,
BILL DANOFF and TAFFY NIVERT

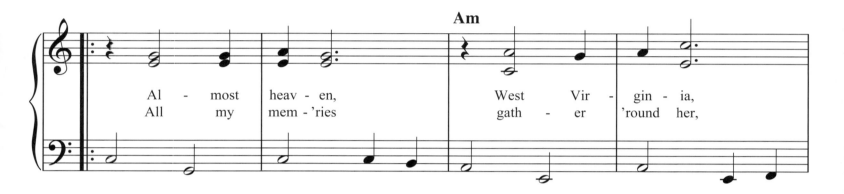

Al - most heav - en,   West Vir - gin - ia,
All my mem - 'ries   gath - er 'round her,

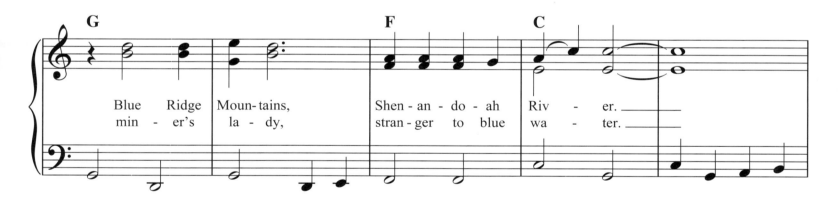

Blue Ridge Moun - tains,   Shen - an - do - ah Riv - er. _____
min - er's la - dy,   stran - ger to blue wa - ter. _____

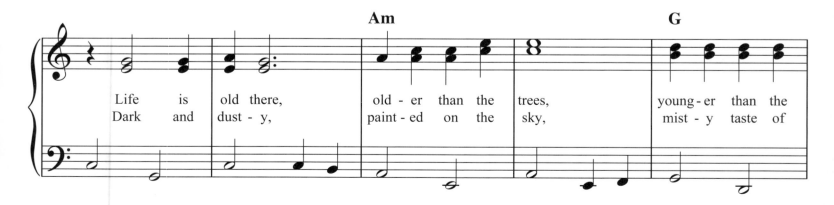

Life is old there,   old - er than the trees,   young - er than the
Dark and dust - y,   paint - ed on the sky,   mist - y taste of

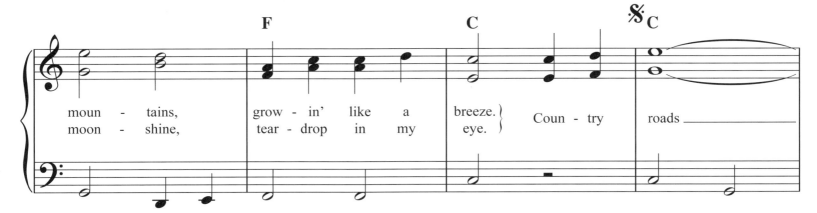

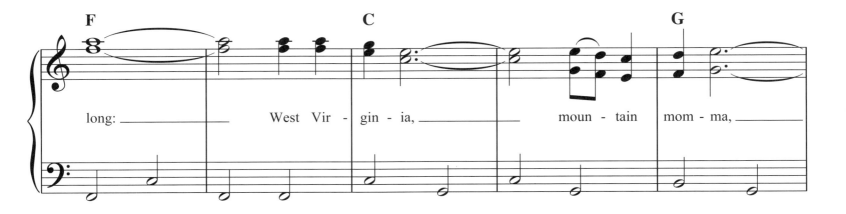

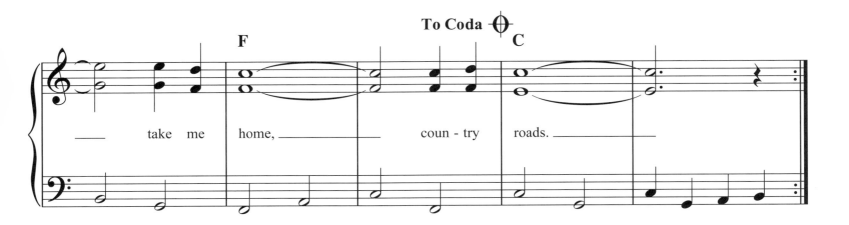

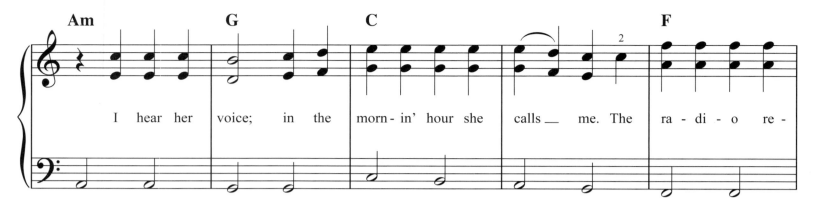

I hear her voice; in the morn-in' hour she calls __ me. The ra - di - o re -

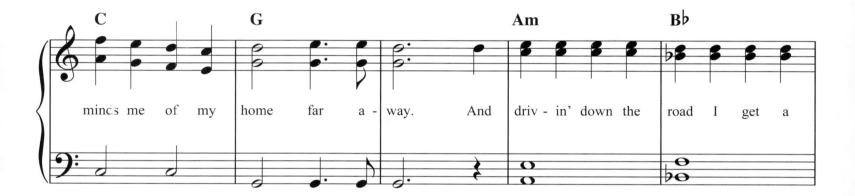

minds me of my home far a - way. And driv-in' down the road I get a

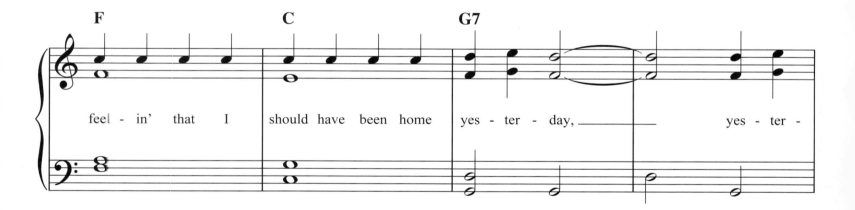

feel - in' that I should have been home yes - ter - day, _____ yes - ter -

day. _____ Coun - try

roads. _____

PEACEFUL EASY FEELING

Words and Music by
JACK TEMPCHIN

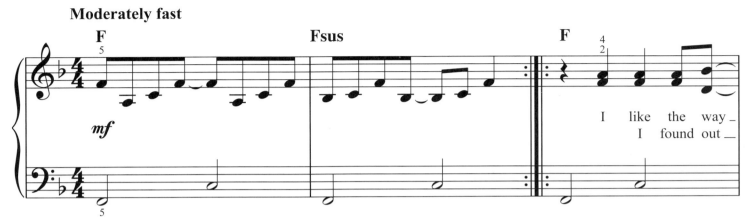

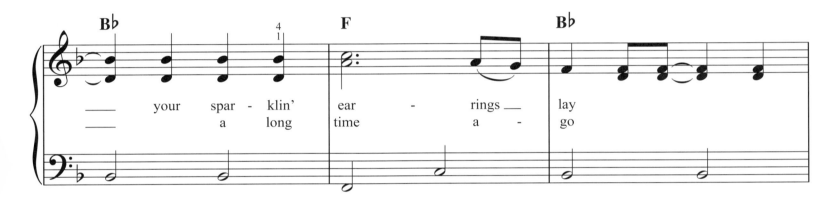

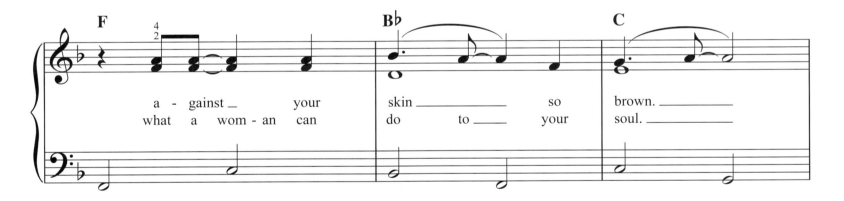

des - ert ___ to - night, with a bil - lion
an - y - way, ___ you don't al - read - y

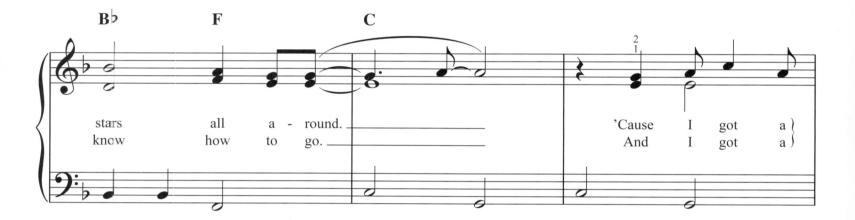

stars all a - round. ___ 'Cause I got a
know how to go. ___ And I got a

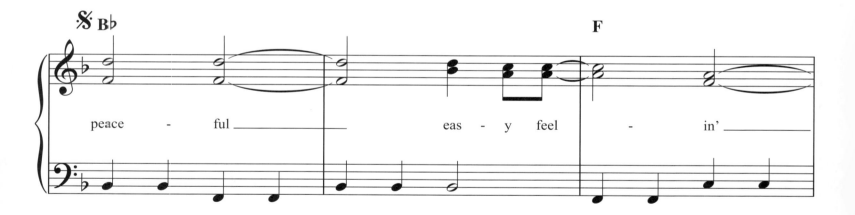

peace - ful ___ eas - y feel - in' ___

___ and I know you won't ___ let me

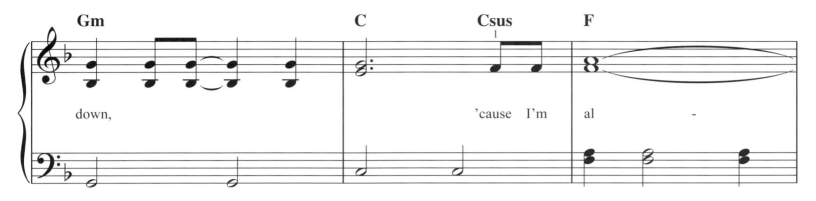

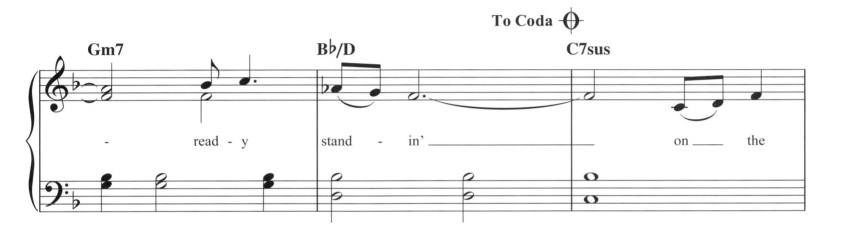

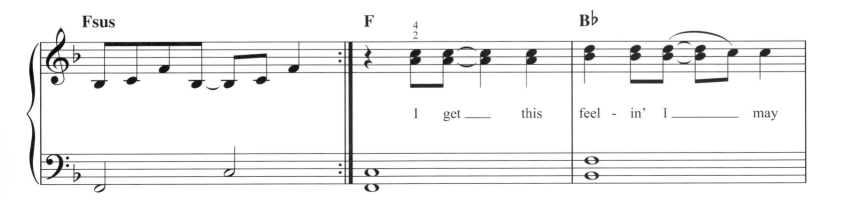

know _____ you

as a lov -

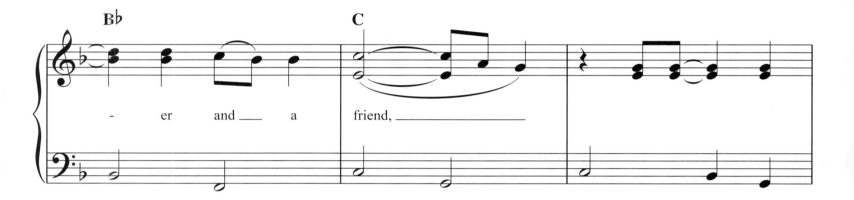

- er and ___ a

friend, _____

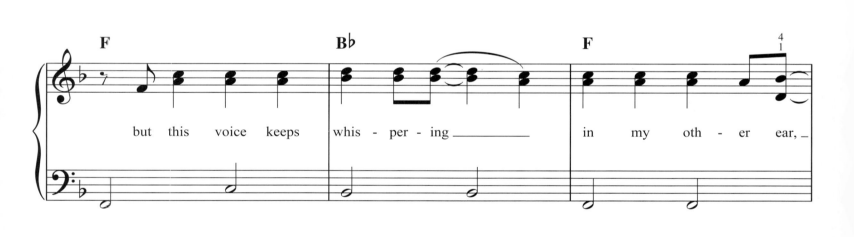

but this voice keeps

whis - per - ing _____

in my oth - er ear, _

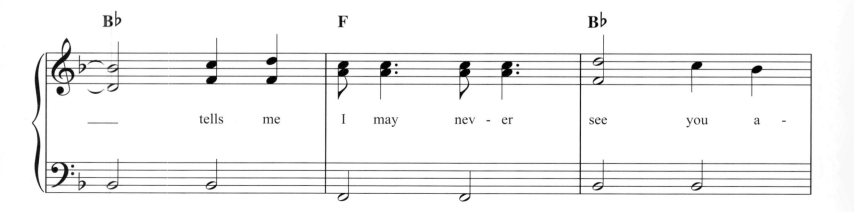

___ tells me

I may nev - er

see you a -

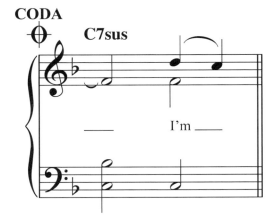

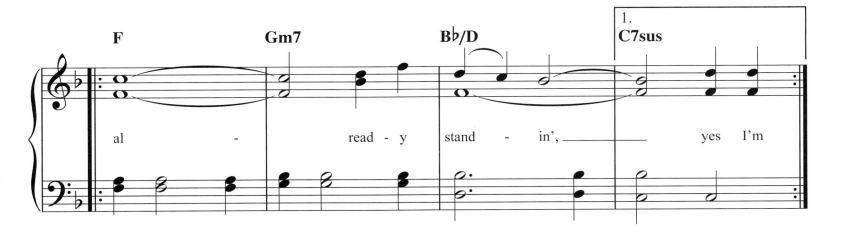

WE WILL ROCK YOU

Words and Music by
BRIAN MAY

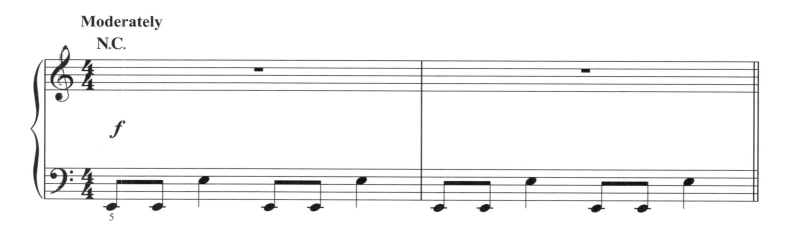

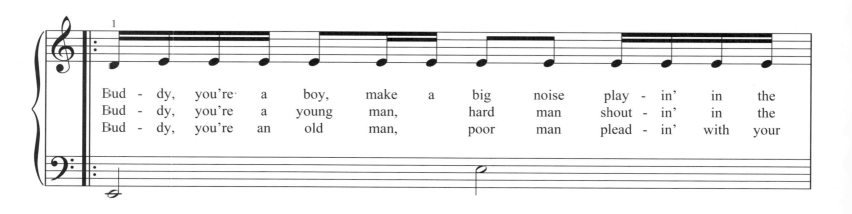

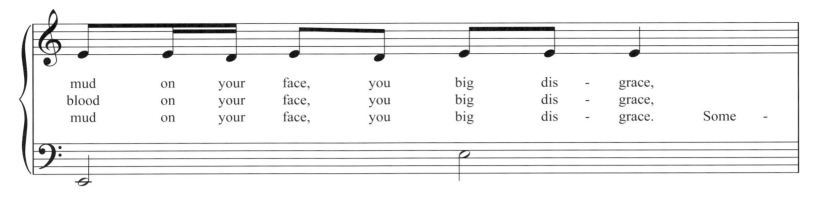

mud on your face, you big dis - grace,
blood on your face, you big dis - grace,
mud on your face, you big dis - grace. Some -

kick - in' your can all o - ver the place. Sing - in'
wav - in' your ban - ner all o - ver the place. Sing - in'
bod - y bet - ter put you back in - to your place. Sing - in'

we will, we will rock you. _____ We will, we will

1., 2.

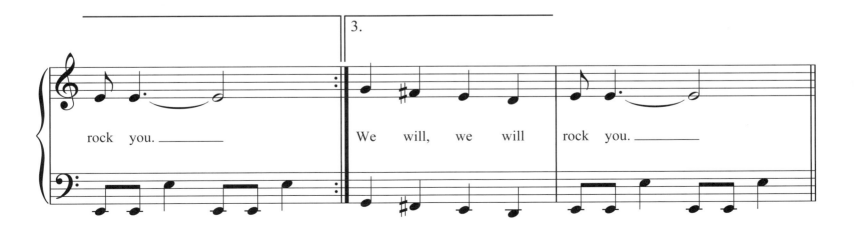

rock you. _____ We will, we will rock you. _____

3.

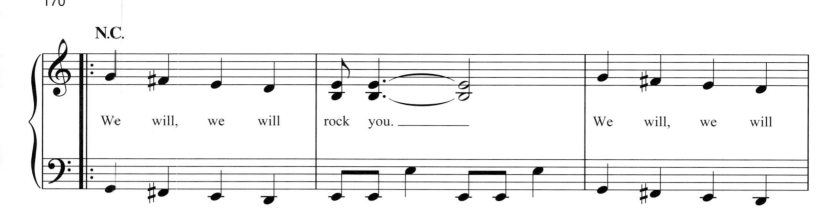

We will, we will rock you. _____ We will, we will

rock you. _____

PIANO MAN

Words and Music by
BILLY JOEL

Moderately

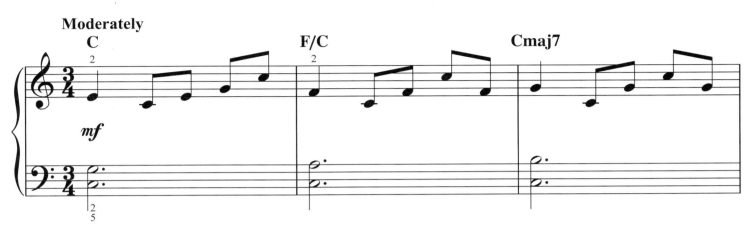

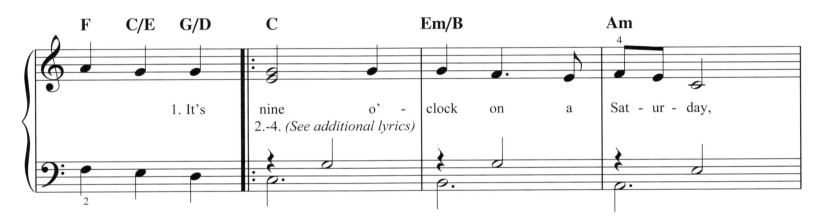

1. It's nine o'- clock on a Sat - ur - day,
2.-4. *(See additional lyrics)*

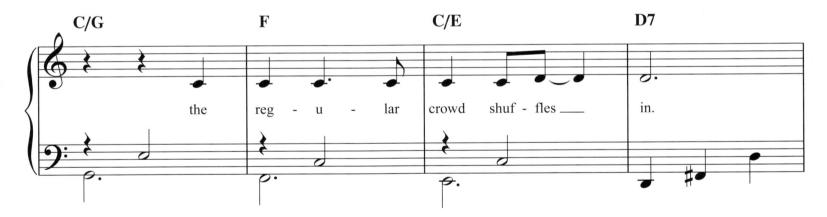

the reg - u - lar crowd shuf - fles ___ in.

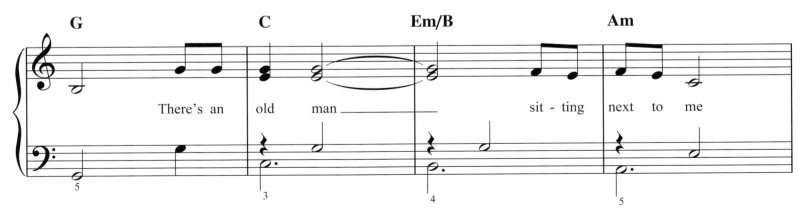

There's an old man ___ sit - ting next to me

172

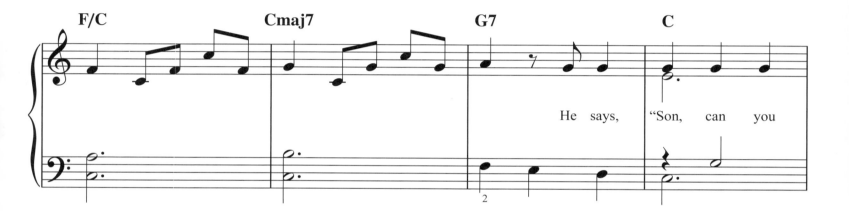

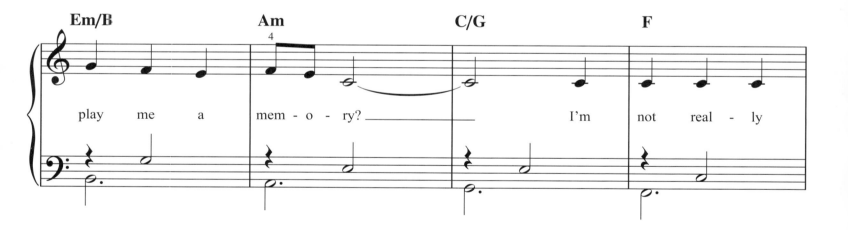

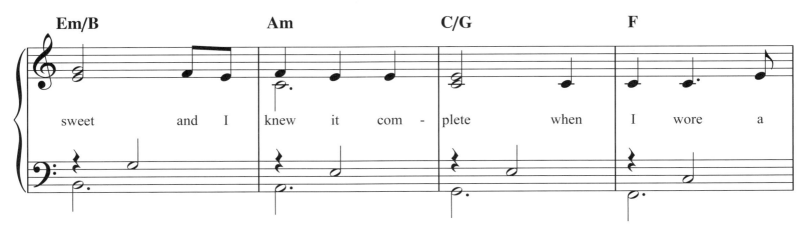

sweet and I knew it com - plete when I wore a

young - er man's clothes."

Chorus

Da da

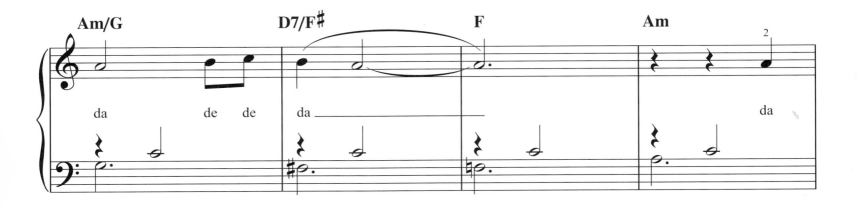

da de de da da

da da

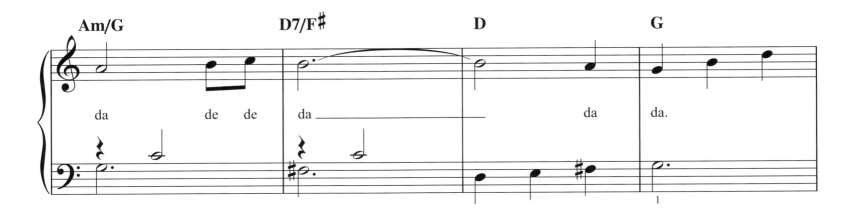

da de de da da da.

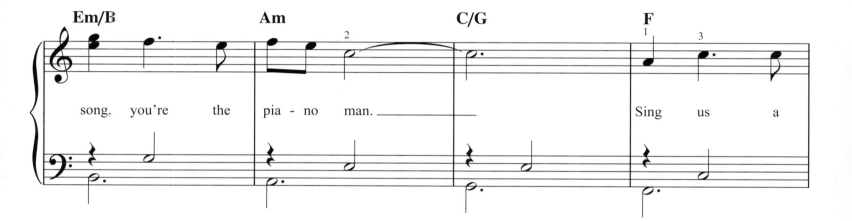

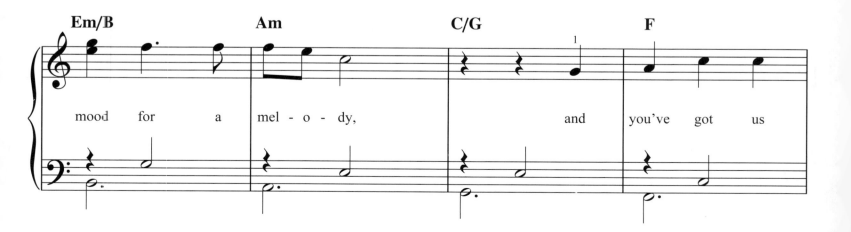

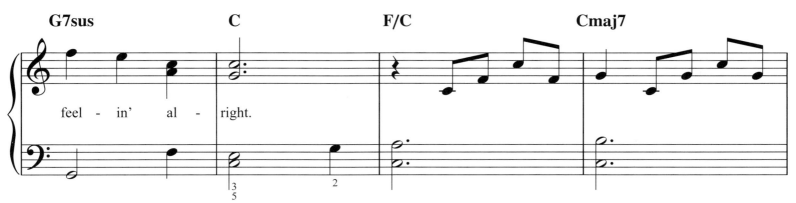

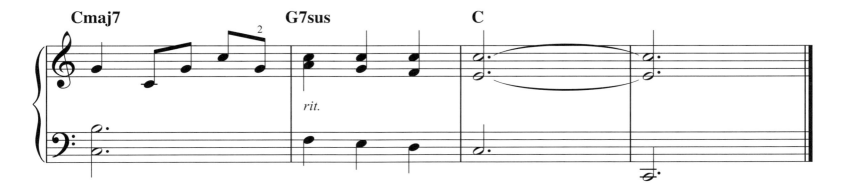

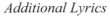

Additional Lyrics

2. Now John at the bar is a friend of mine,
   He gets me my drinks for free,
   And he's quick with a joke or to light up your smoke,
   But there's someplace that he'd rather be.
   He says, "Bill, I believe this is killing me,"
   As a smile ran away from his face.
   "Well, I'm sure that I could be a movie star
   If I could get out of this place."
   Chorus

3. Now Paul is a real estate novelist
   Who never had time for a wife,
   And he's talkin' with Davy who's still in the Navy
   And probably will be for life.
   And the waitress is practicing politics
   As the businessmen slowly get stoned.
   Yes, they're sharing a drink they call loneliness,
   But it's better than drinkin' alone.
   Chorus

4. It's a pretty good crowd for a Saturday,
   And the manager gives me a smile
   'Cause he knows that it's me they've been comin' to see
   To forget about life for a while.
   And the piano sounds like a carnival,
   And the microphone smells like a beer,
   And they sit at the bar and put bread in my jar
   And say, "Man, what are you doin' here?"
   Chorus

SOMEWHERE, MY LOVE

Lara's Theme from DOCTOR ZHIVAGO

Lyric by PAUL FRANCIS WEBSTER
Music by MAURICE JARRE

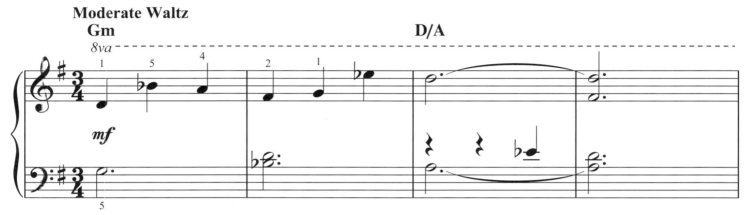

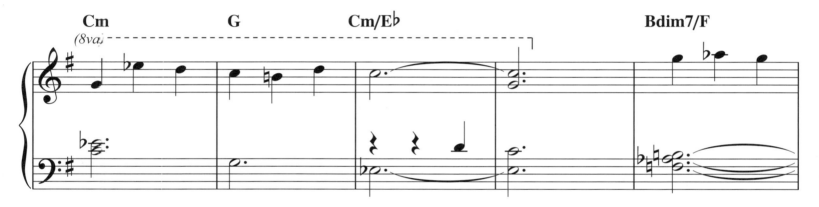

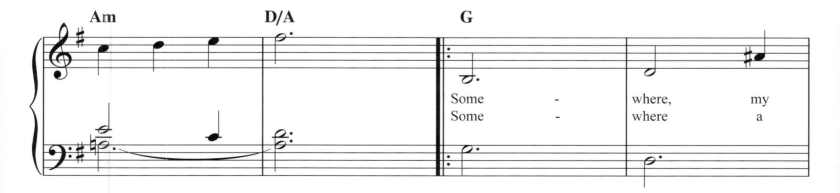

Some - where, my
Some - where a

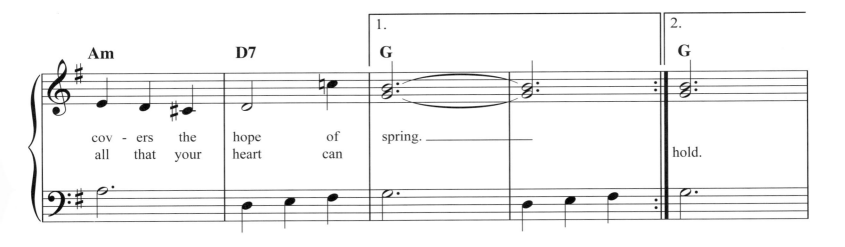

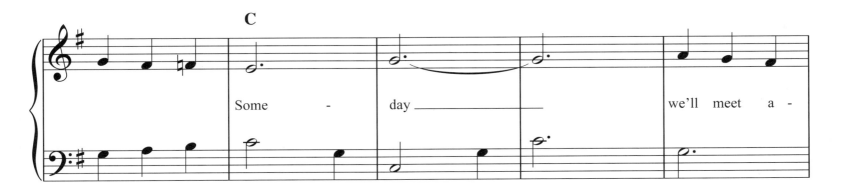

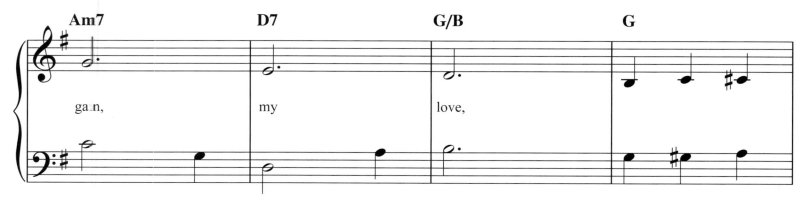

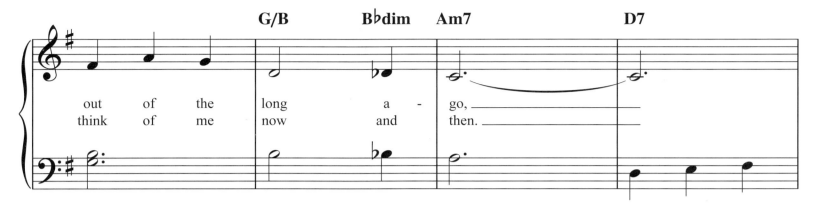

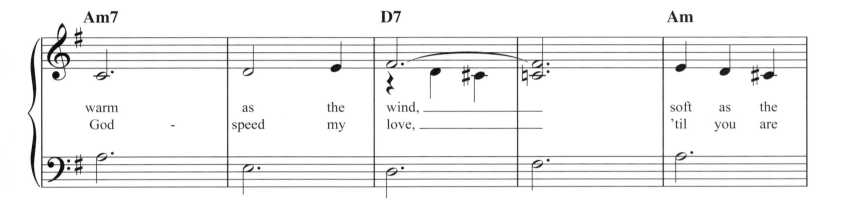

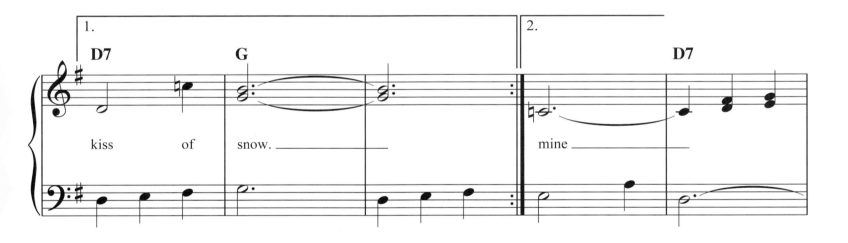

SUMMERTIME
from PORGY AND BESS®

Music and Lyrics by GEORGE GERSHWIN,
DuBOSE and DOROTHY HEYWARD
and IRA GERSHWIN

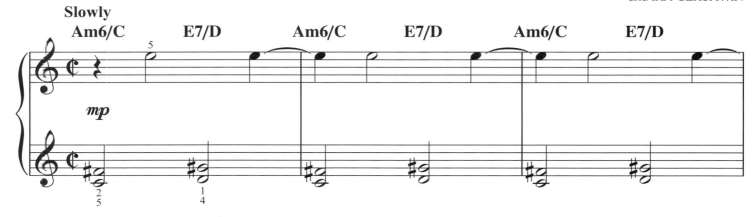

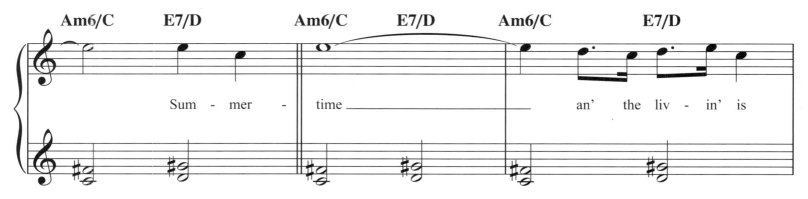

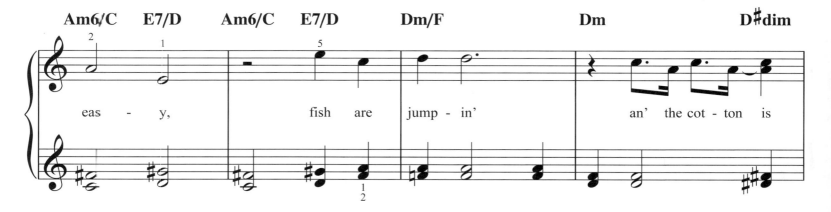

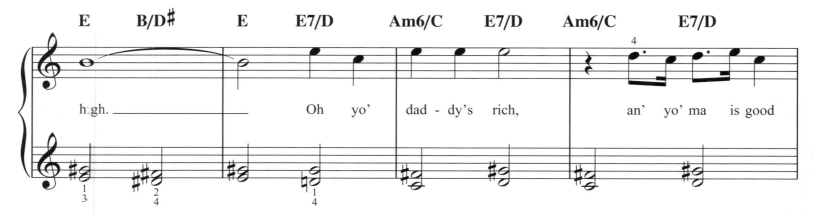

181

look - in', so hush, lit - tle ba - by, don' — you

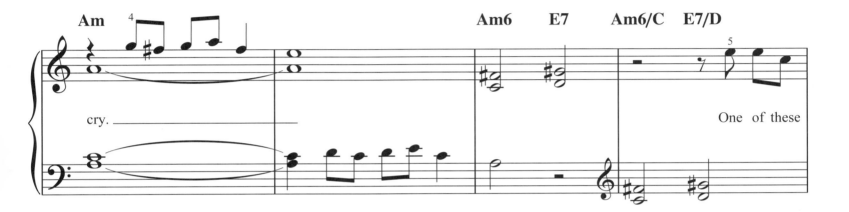

cry. _____ One of these

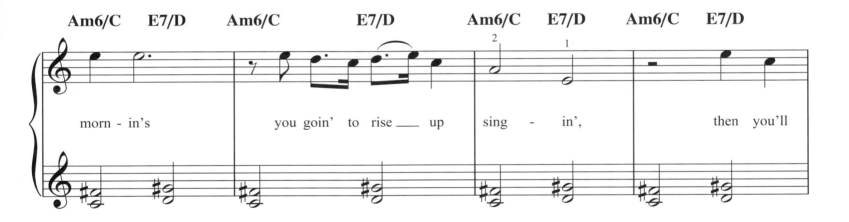

morn - in's you goin' to rise ___ up sing - in', then you'll

spread yo' wings an' you'll take ___ the sky. _____

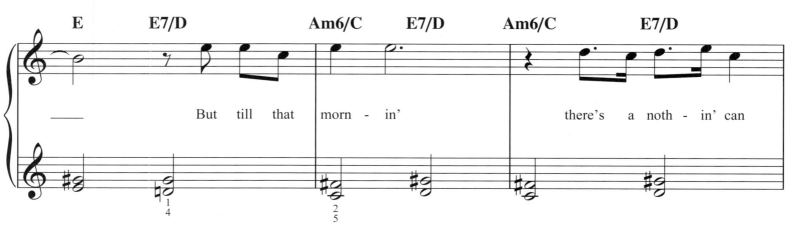

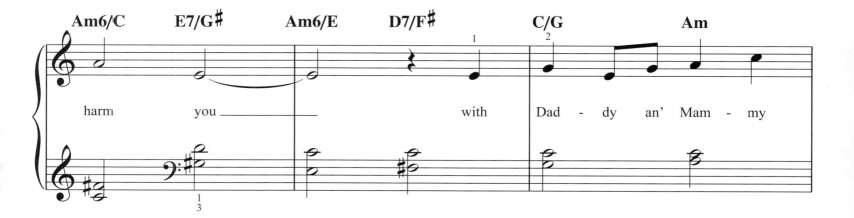

STAND BY ME

Words and Music by JERRY LEIBER,
MIKE STOLLER and BEN E. KING

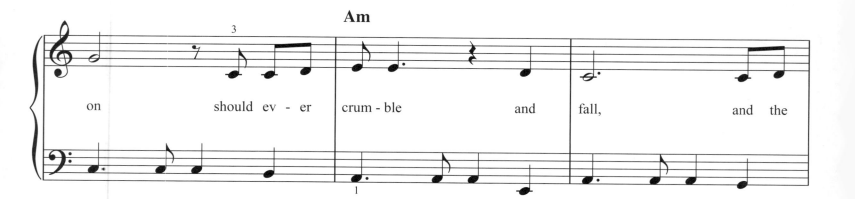

185

moun - tains _____ should fall ____ to the sea, _____

no, I won't _ be a - fraid, _ no, I won't ____ shed a

tear just as long _ as you stand, _ stand by me.

Dar - ling, stand _____ by

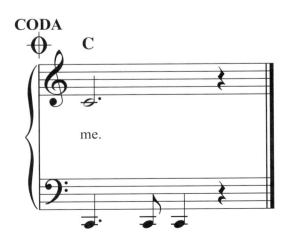

me.

THE WINDMILLS OF YOUR MIND

Theme from THE THOMAS CROWN AFFAIR

Words by ALAN and MARILYN BERGMAN
Music by MICHEL LEGRAND

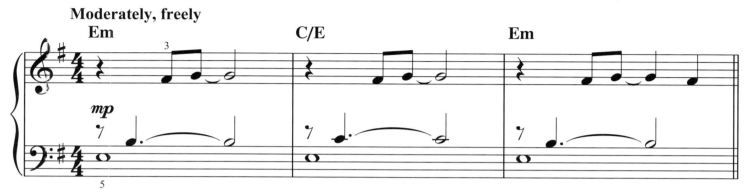

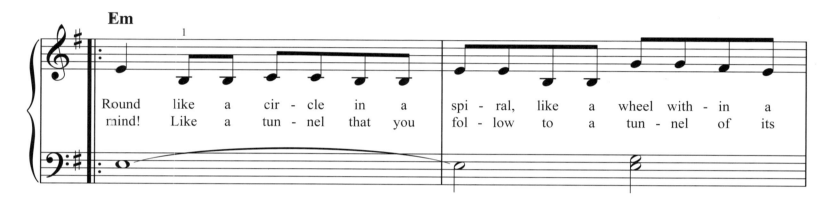

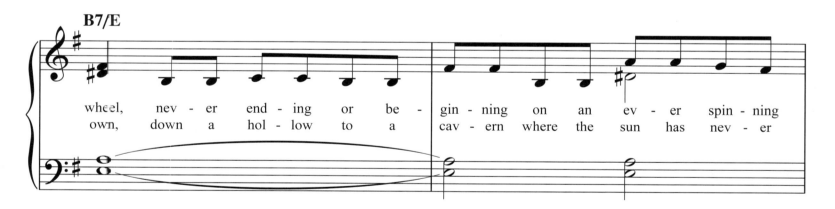

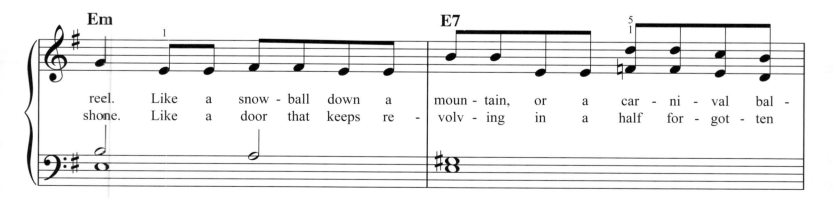

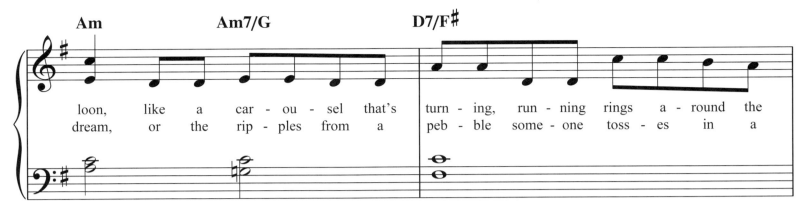

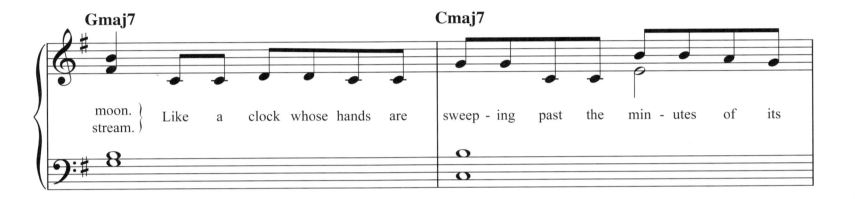

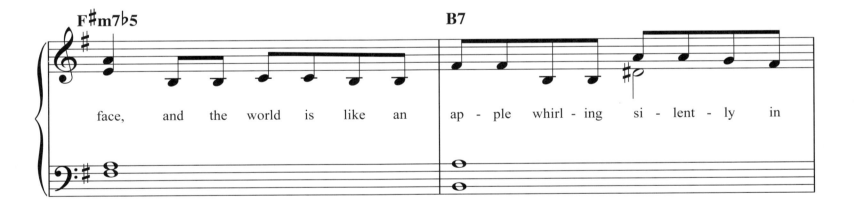

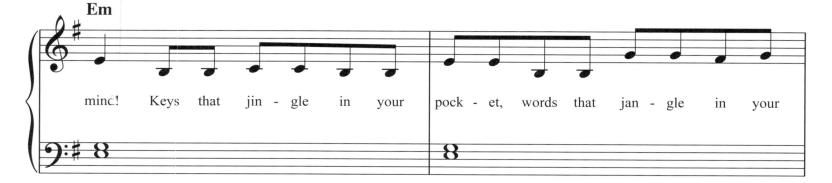

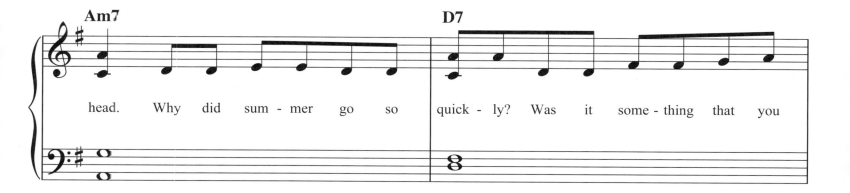

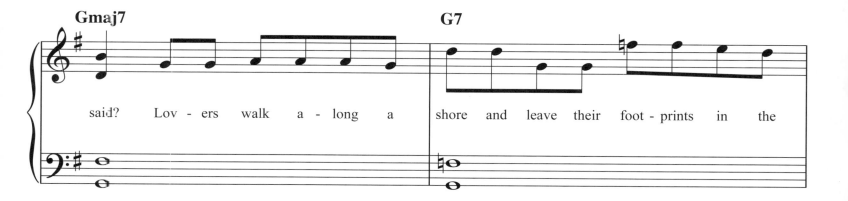

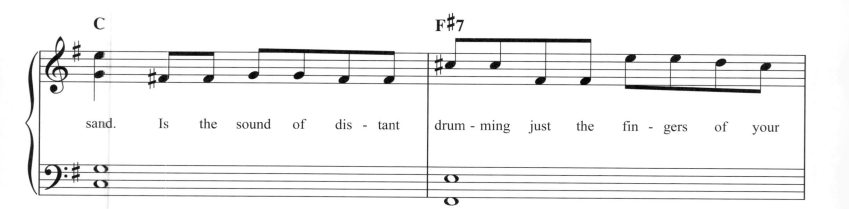

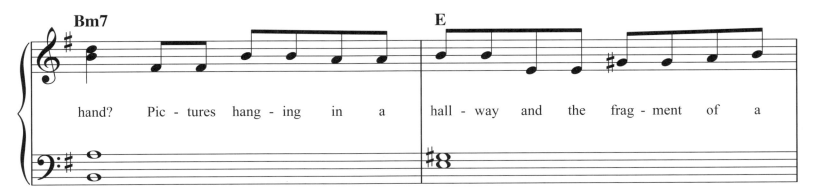

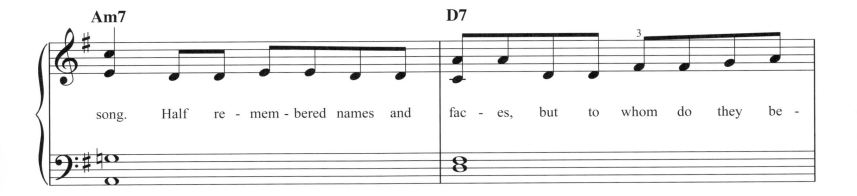

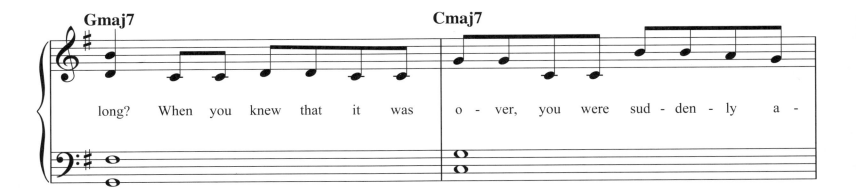

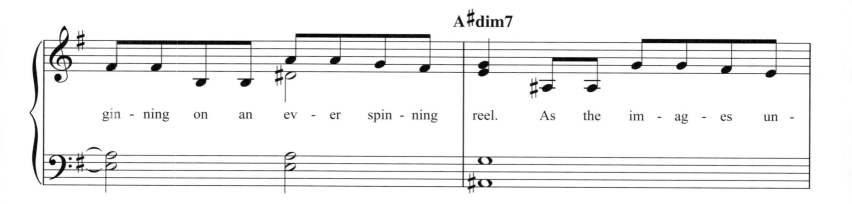

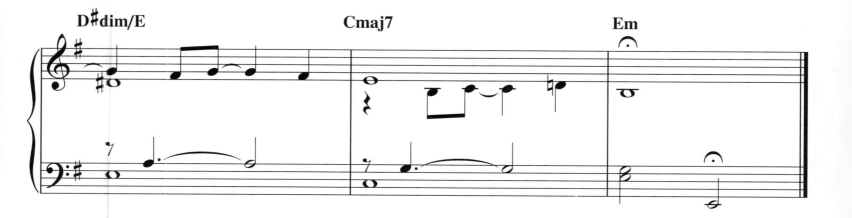

TOO LITTLE TIME
Love Theme from THE GLENN MILLER STORY

Words by DON RAYE
Music by HENRY MANCINI

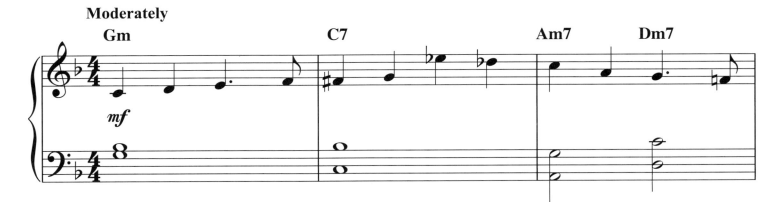

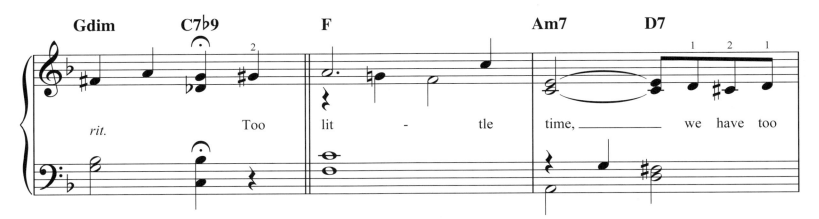

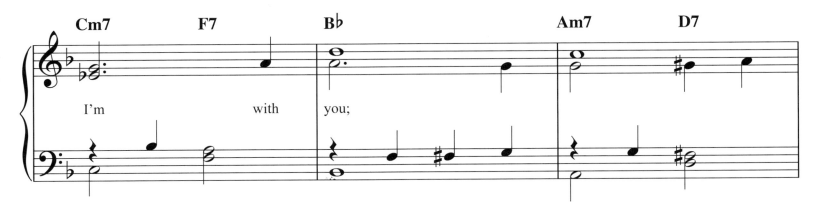

no — time for us to love and laugh e - nough, ____

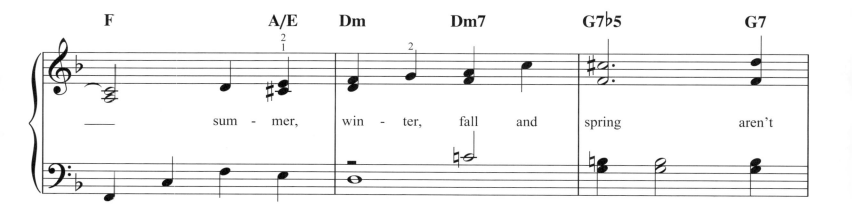

____ sum - mer, win - ter, fall and spring aren't

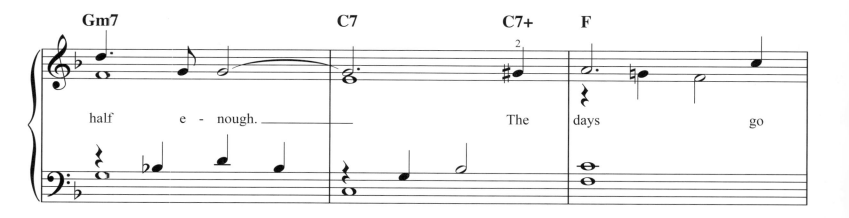

half e - nough. ____ The days go

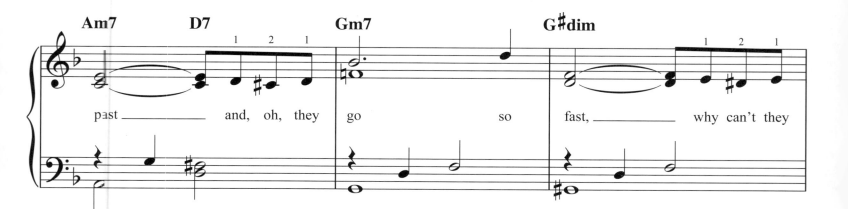

past ____ and, oh, they go so fast, ____ why can't they

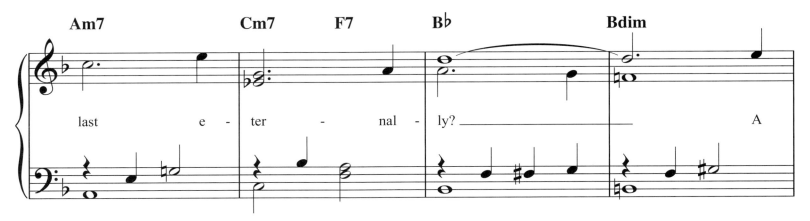

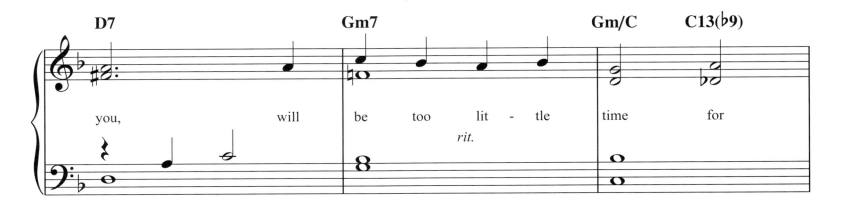

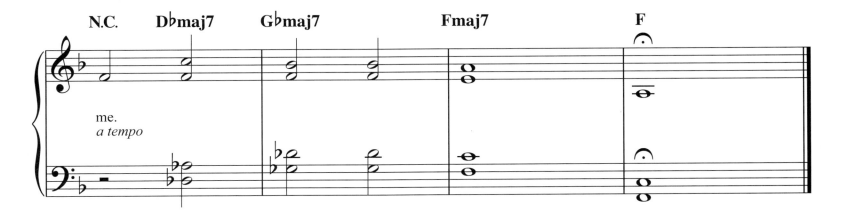

UNCHAINED MELODY

from the Motion Picture UNCHAINED
featured in the Motion Picture GHOST

Lyric by HY ZARET
Music by ALEX NORTH

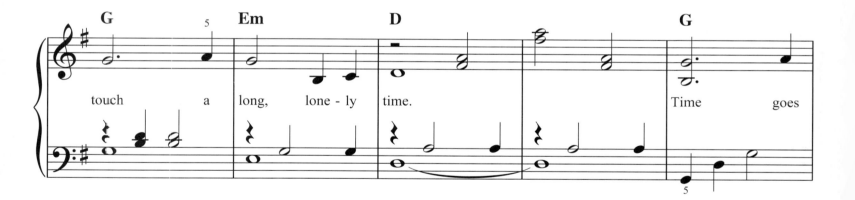

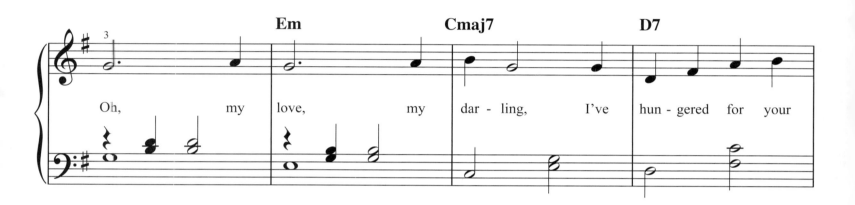

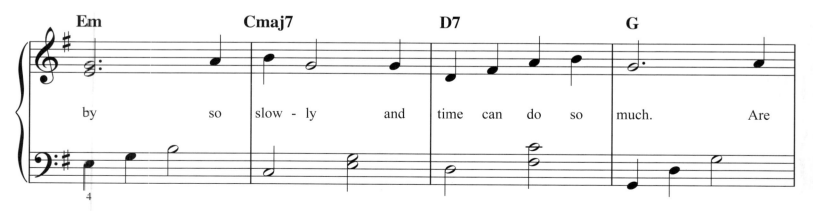

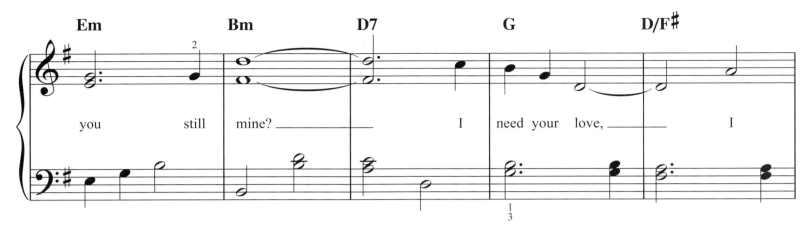

you   still   mine? _____ _____   I   need your love, _____   I

need your love. _____ _____   God   speed your love   to   me.

Slightly faster

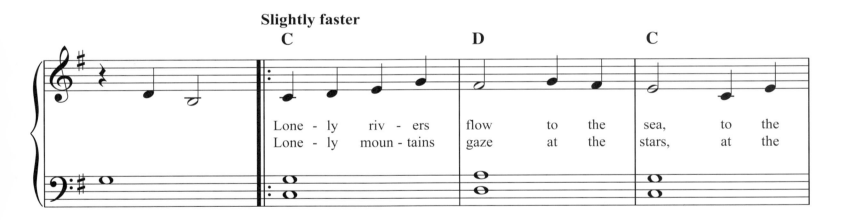

Lone - ly   riv - ers   flow   to   the   sea,   to   the
Lone - ly   moun - tains   gaze   at   the   stars,   at   the

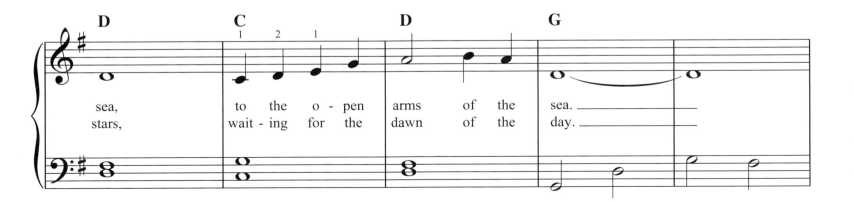

sea,   to   the o - pen   arms   of   the   sea. _____
stars,   wait - ing   for   the   dawn   of   the   day. _____

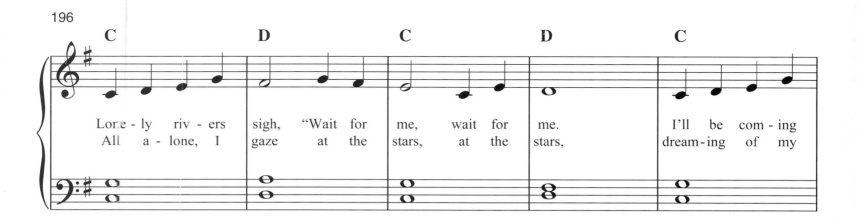

C   **D**   **C**   **D**   **C**

Lone - ly riv - ers sigh, "Wait for me, wait for me.   I'll be com - ing
All a - lone, I gaze at the stars, at the stars,   dream - ing of my

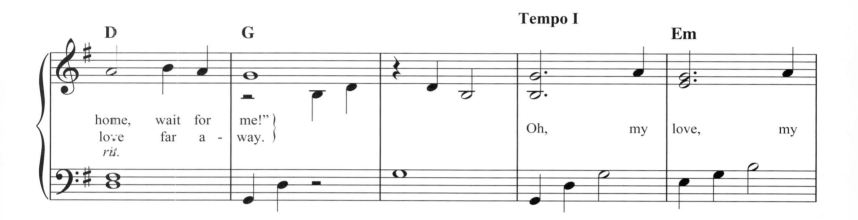

D   **G**   **Tempo I**   **Em**

home, wait for me!"   Oh, my love, my
love far a - way.   *rit.*

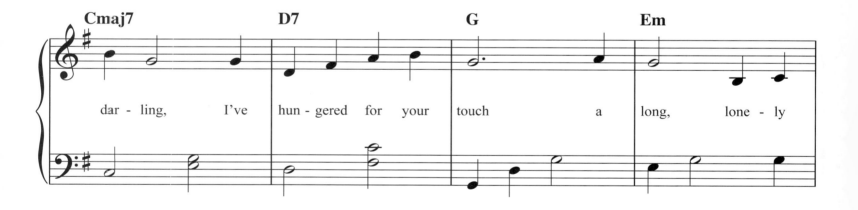

Cmaj7   **D7**   **G**   **Em**

dar - ling, I've hun - gered for your touch a long, lone - ly

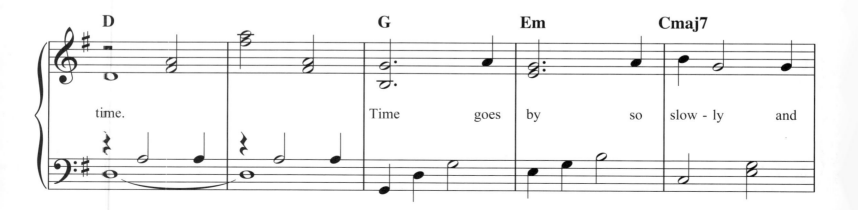

D   **G**   **Em**   **Cmaj7**

time.   Time goes by so slow - ly and

time can do so much. Are you still mine? _____ I

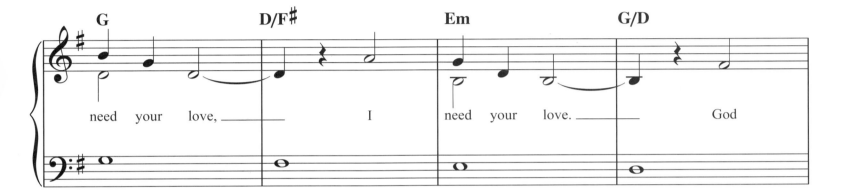

need your love, _____ I need your love. _____ God

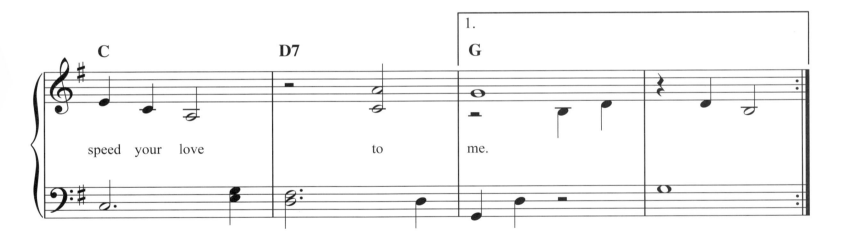

speed your love to me.

me. *dim. e rit.*

WHAT A WONDERFUL WORLD

Words and Music by GEORGE DAVID WEISS
and BOB THIELE

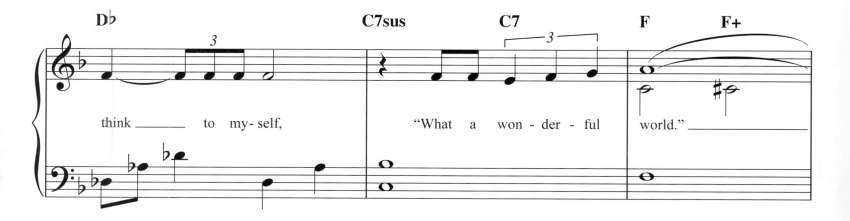

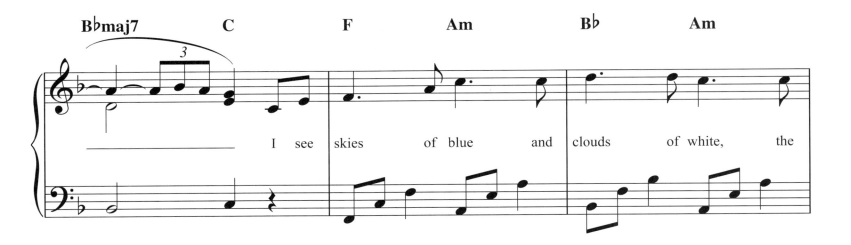

I see skies of blue and clouds of white, the

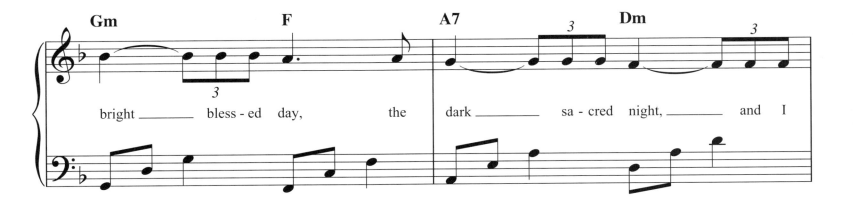

bright _____ bless - ed day, the dark _____ sa - cred night, _____ and I

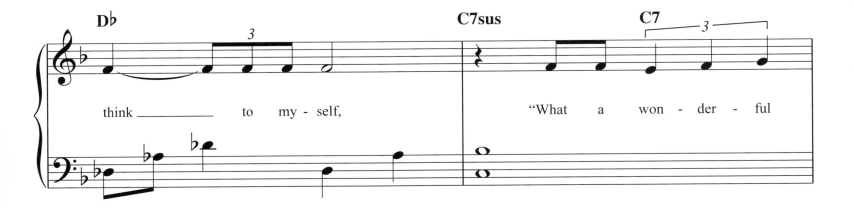

think _____ to my - self, "What a won - der - ful

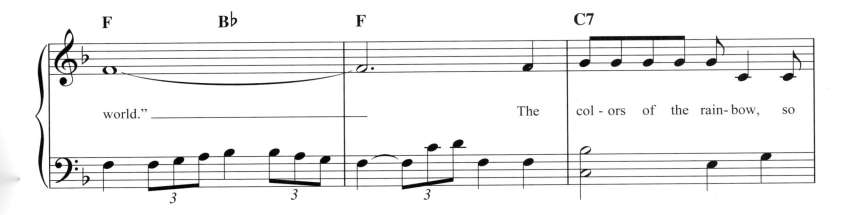

world." _____ The col - ors of the rain - bow, so

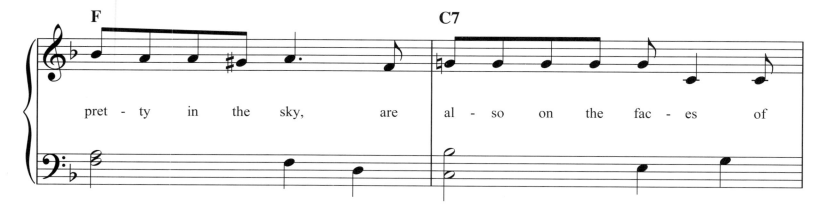

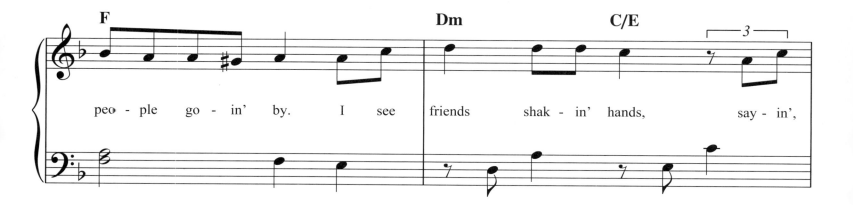

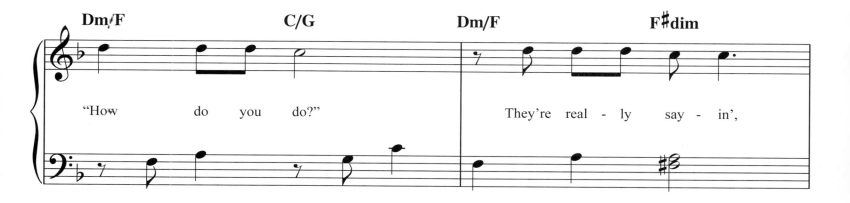

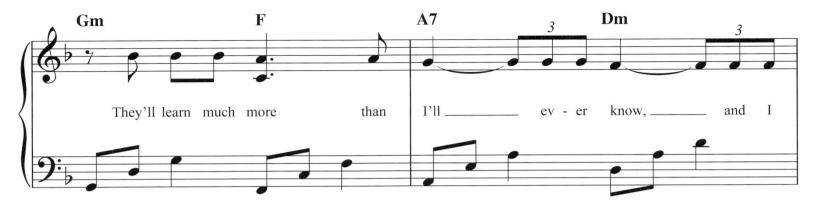

They'll learn much more than I'll _____ ev - er know, _____ and I

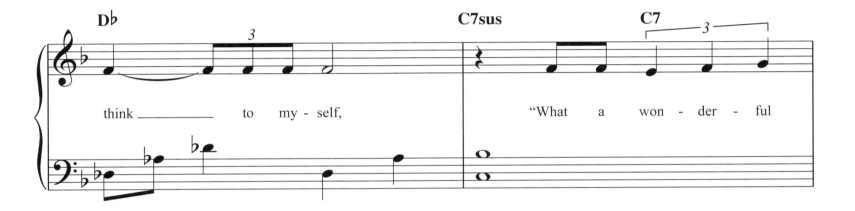

think _____ to my - self, "What a won - der - ful

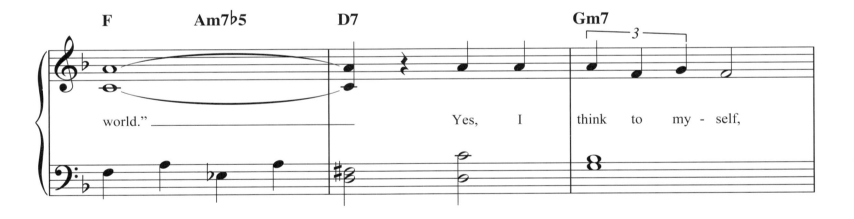

world." _____ Yes, I think to my - self,

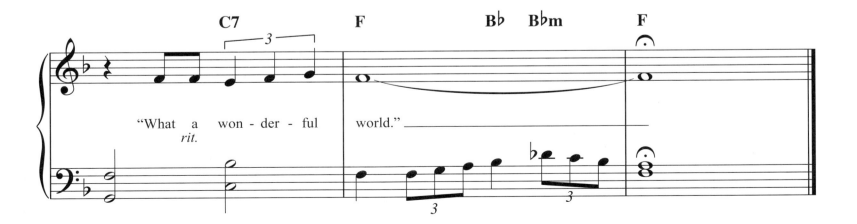

"What a won - der - ful world." _____

rit.

YESTERDAY

Words and Music by JOHN LENNON
and PAUL McCARTNEY

Moderately, with expression

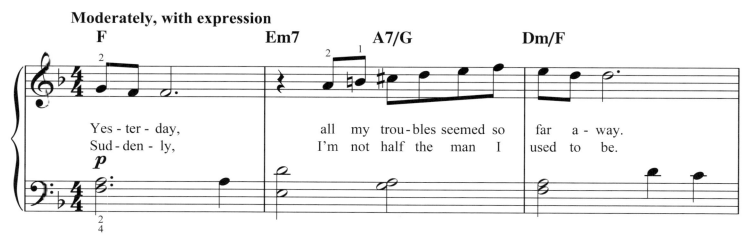

Yes - ter - day, all my trou - bles seemed so far a - way.
Sud - den - ly, I'm not half the man I used to be.

Now it looks as though they're here to stay. __ Oh, I be - lieve __ in
There's a shad - ow hang - ing o - ver me. __ Oh, yes - ter - day __ came

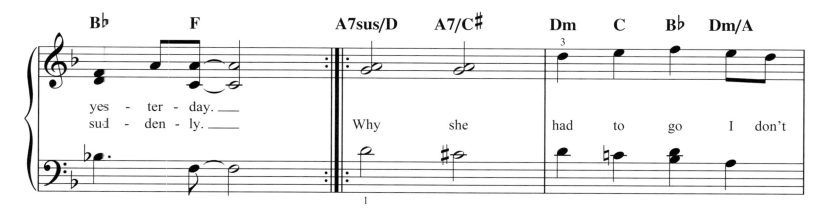

yes - ter - day. __
sud - den - ly. __ Why she had to go I don't

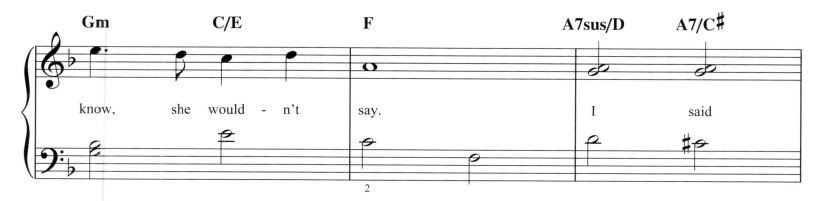

know, she would - n't say. I said

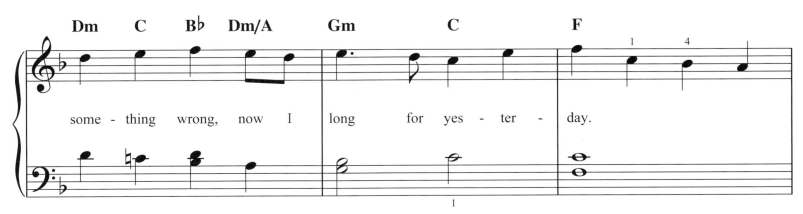

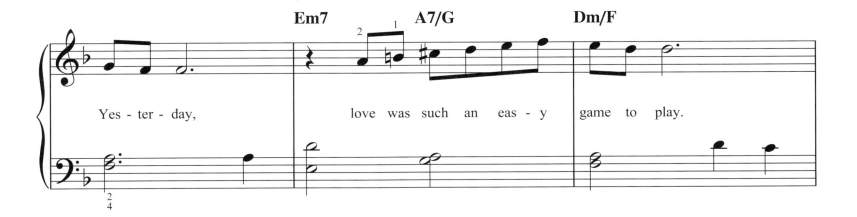

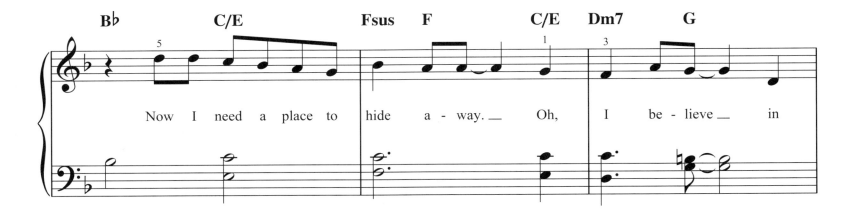

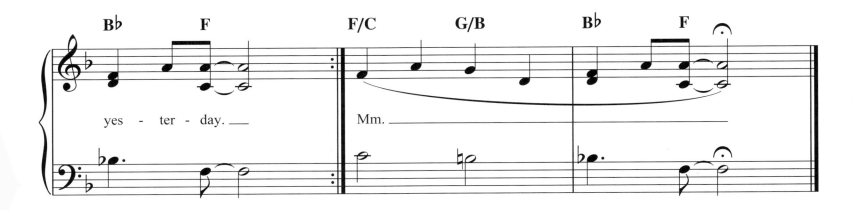

YOUR SONG

Words and Music by ELTON JOHN
and BERNIE TAUPIN

It's a lit - tle bit   fun - ny,
If I were a   sculp - tor,
I sat on a   roof

this feel - ing in - side; _____
but then a - gain,   no, _____
and kicked off the   moss; _____

I'm not   one of
or a man   who makes
a   few of the

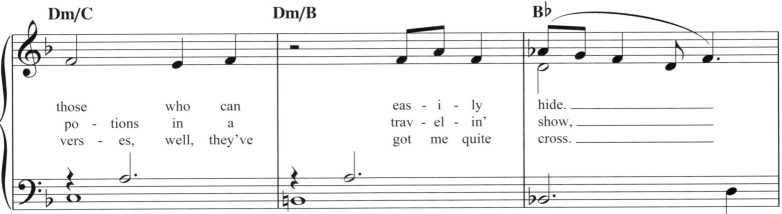

those who can
po - tions in a
vers - es, well, they've
eas - i - ly
trav - el - in'
got me quite
hide. _____
show, _____
cross. _____

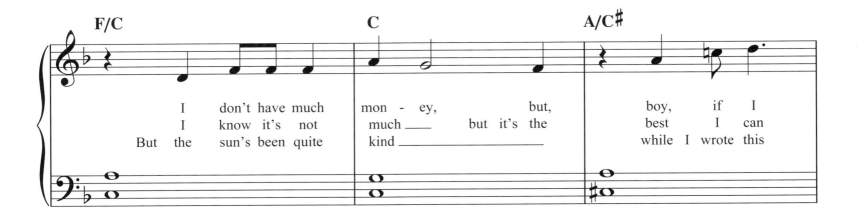

I don't have much
I know it's not
But the sun's been quite
mon - ey, but,
much _____ but it's the
kind _____
boy, if I
best I can
while I wrote this

did, _____
do. _____
song; _____
I'd buy a big
My gift is my
it's for peo - ple like
house where _____
song and _____
you that _____

we both __ could
live. _____

this one's __ for you.)
keep it ____ turned on.)

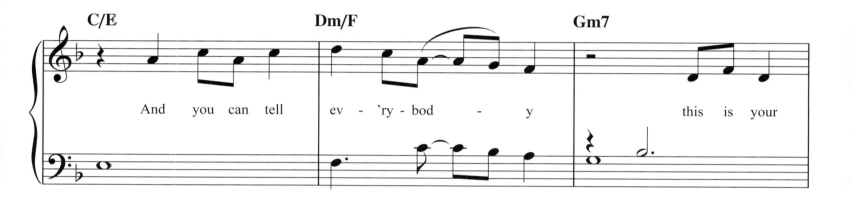

And you can tell ev - 'ry - bod - y this is your

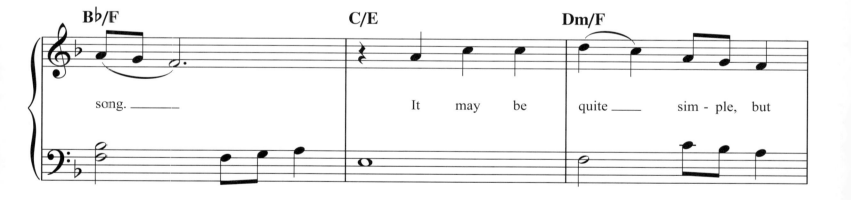

song. _____ It may be quite ____ sim - ple, but

To Coda $\oplus$

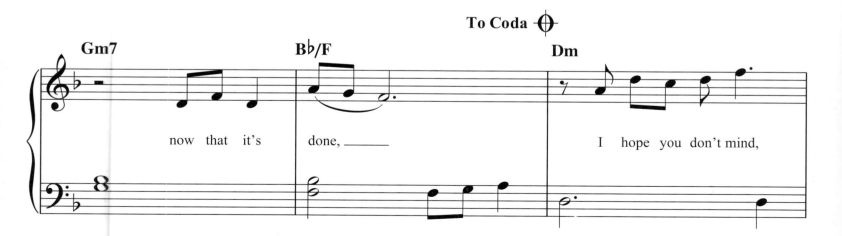

now that it's done, _____ I hope you don't mind,

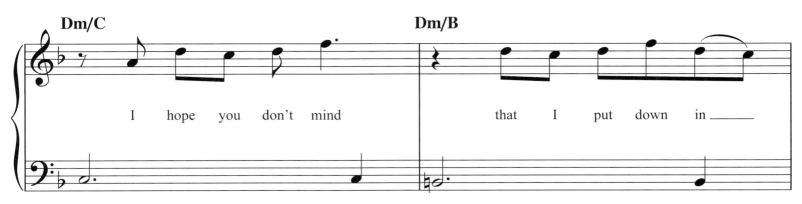

I hope you don't mind that I put down in _____

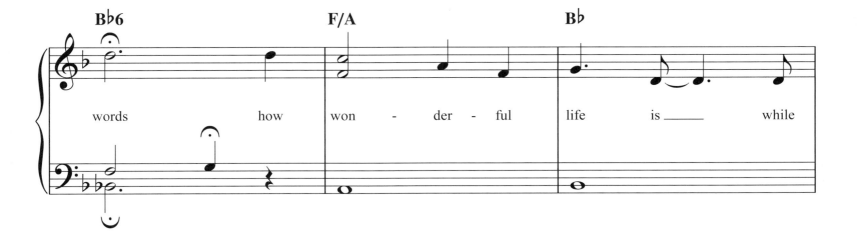

words how won - der - ful life is _____ while

D.S. al Coda
(take 2nd ending)

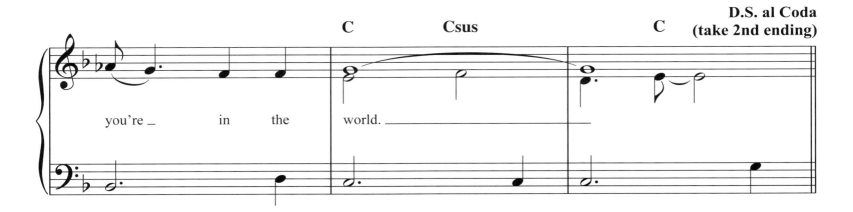

you're ___ in the world. _____

I hope you don't mind, I hope you don't mind that I put down in ___

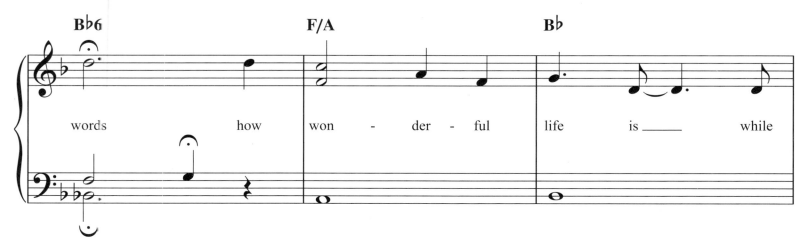

words how won - der - ful life is ____ while

you're _ in the world.

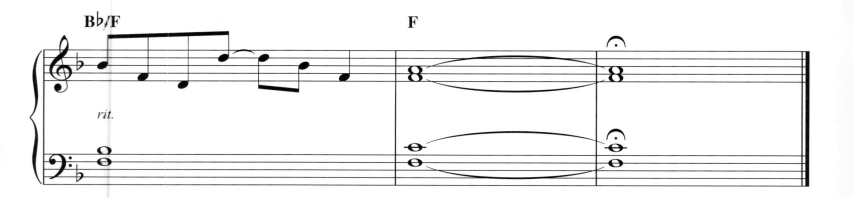

rit.